✝

More Than Your
BUSINESS CARD

WHAT PEOPLE ARE SAYING ABOUT
MORE THAN YOUR BUSINESS CARD

"This is a must-read for every leader wanting to make a Kingdom impact. What does it mean to be called to business? How does a leader overcome obstacles and answer tough questions in a marketplace context? Garth Jestley provides a solid scriptural perspective and engaging stories from his own experience as a C-suite leader. This is a book that will anchor your true identity as a follower of Christ and help you realize your Kingdom potential using your platform as a marketplace leader."

Nathan Hildebrandt
LeaderImpact Global

"I have always been acutely aware that in my career as a marketplace leader, God was leading, guiding, and protecting me. It wasn't until my early fifties I asked God the 'why' question; what was God's purpose in blessing me with a position and title of influence? Answering that question took me on a life-changing journey that resulted in the most fulfilling years of my career. Garth writes from his own journey and experience. You will find he both challenges and equips you so that you too can experience your true calling as a Christian marketplace leader."

Don Van Meer
Retired President/CEO of Carswell, a Thomson Reuters business

"Marrying his tender relationship with Jesus with senior business experience, Garth Jestley is perfectly equipped to write this quintessential handbook on living our Christian faith in the marketplace. In the early 2000s, we served together on the board of one of Canada's leading charities and Garth's God-given wisdom and financial acumen were crucial to navigating the ministry through an existential threat and into its thriving future. Garth's initial encounter with Jesus mirrored the moment my life pivoted dramatically. As I answer my call to practice law while serving Christian ministries, *More Than Your Business Card* challenges me to sharpen my focus on Jesus and shine His light every day."

Stevan Novoselac
Chair, Boards of Directors, Crossroads Christian Communications Inc.
and YesTV, Burlington, Canada, and President, Deacon Board of Directors,
Church on the Queensway, Toronto, Canada

"Garth has captured the very essence of being in his book *More Than Your Business Card*. As you read, you will find yourself in the pages and feel confident you are not alone. He challenges us in our thinking while at the same time providing practical ways to help us on our journey. As a woman who has held many leadership positions, I have often been challenged about my beliefs and my attitude toward business. This book reminds me I am not alone. It confirms life is not a destination; it is a journey. I am pleased to recommend this book to leaders everywhere. By reading and applying it, you will be that much richer."

Irene E. Pfeiffer, CM
Member of the Order of Canada and Chair of Teen Challenge Canada

"Being Garth's pastor for over twenty years, I can say he lives this book! As a successful business leader, Garth explains why and how Christians in leadership must use their professional platform to make Jesus known to their peers. I wholeheartedly agree and commend this book to every leader desiring to follow Jesus in the marketplace."

Steve Long
Senior Leader, Catch the Fire Church Toronto

"Garth's remarkable marketplace career, his faith journey, his deep grasp of apologetics, and his experience with the LeaderImpact ministry give him the unique credibility to write such a book. I personally know him to be not only a seasoned practitioner but also an excellent communicator. Whether you need to get off the sidelines or the fence, this book will provide encouragement and practical steps."

Jacques Lapointe
Former CEO of GSK Canada and UK
and Former Chair of Teen Challenge Canada,
Corporate Director and Business Owner

"In *More Than Your Business Card,* Garth Jestley weaves the story of his life experiences as a leader at the most senior levels of business together with his faith in Jesus Christ. That faith has enabled him to deal with the inevitable challenges we all face in marketplace leadership. This book provides the reader with the tools to walk fearlessly in their business calling while demonstrating their God-given abilities as committed believers in Jesus Christ. Having known Garth and his wife, Mary, for nearly forty years, I can attest to his strong faith in God and his business acumen. He has been an example to me and other business leaders around the world. I am certain readers will come away from this book surer of God's call on their own lives, especially in the marketplace."

John Carmichael, ICD.D
CEO & Registrar, Ontario Motor Vehicle Industry Council,
Corporate Director and former Member of Parliament

"*More Than Your Business Card* is a powerful reminder of what is real and what is enduring. Garth Jestley has clearly articulated the 'why' that has driven him to lead in business from an eternal perspective. This 'why' has enabled him to deal with the cut and thrust of the business environment and given him a purpose beyond making money and advancing himself. As I read through these chapters, I was constantly reminded that the marketplace can be a noble venue to experience fulfillment and make a meaningful impact. I have lived my life as a Christian in the marketplace, and this book has reminded me of the simple truths for which I must keep standing. I put this book down, filled with renewed hope for what is possible. I am sure you will too."

Kevin Bailey, AM
Member of the Order of Australia, founder of The Money Managers Ltd,
co-founder of Shadforth Financial Group,
and former Director of the Sovereign Wealth Fund of Timor-Leste

"'If we were put on trial for being a follower of Jesus in the marketplace, would there be enough evidence to convict us?' is the very essence of this book. Garth challenges his readers, as he and Mary have challenged themselves, to want the answer to be an emphatic *yes*. *More Than Your Business Card* should motivate believers called to business."

Paul Tyers
Managing Director, Wealth Stewards Inc.

"*More Than Your Business Card* is an intelligent and illuminating account of the journey of a business executive called to integrate his Christian faith in the marketplaces of North America and Europe. It is an introspective guidebook filled with practical insights and advice for those who have resolved to apply the principles of Jesus in their business endeavours. For over four decades, I have been edified and encouraged by my friend Garth Jestley. I have learned so much from such a humble, bright, and remarkable human being and gifted business leader."

Dr. Jacques Gauthier
International Jurist and Scholar

"If you are a businessperson or doing other work in the marketplace, there is good news for you. God may well have you there as part of His purpose for your life. In *More Than Your Business Card*, Garth Jestley provides us with a positive perspective on the marketplace as a space where Jesus loves to walk and do business. I find the paradigm both inspiring and challenging. The examples in the book illustrate well what it means to be a witness for Christ in the marketplace. This book is a must-read for marketplace leaders all over the world!"

Professor Delanyo Adadevoh
President, International Leadership Foundation

"Most people have yet to experience God's transformative friendship yet spend so much time and focus at work. As a business veteran himself, Garth articulates the profound opportunity and humbling responsibility we have as marketplace leaders to authentically live and lead by Kingdom values. The call is clear. We can make eternal returns by illuminating the journey to God for our team members, clients and stakeholders."

Donald E. Simmonds
Chairman, The Blyth Group

"I have known Garth Jestley for many years and have witnessed his passion for reaching leaders in business and society generally with the good news of Jesus Christ. These leaders are truly an 'unreached people group' and the best way to impact them with the gospel is through peers who themselves are followers of Jesus. When I launched LeaderImpact in Ontario many years ago, I wish I had had this book. It inspires me and I know it will inspire many other leaders to respond to God's call on them! While written primarily with Christian leaders in mind, *More Than Your Business Card* lends itself to sharing with leaders who are not yet followers of Jesus. Garth's story will be credible with them as will his clear answers to some of the most common objections to the Christian worldview."

Paul Henderson, CM OOnt
Member of the Order of Canada and Order of Ontario and founder of LeaderImpact in Ontario. As a former professional hockey player, Paul scored the series-winning goal in the 1972 Summit Series between Canada and the former Soviet Union, which was voted the "sports moment of the century" by The Canadian Press.

"If as a Christian businessperson you have ever doubted your contribution to kingdom work compared to your theologically trained church pastor or the servant-heart of a Christ-filled employee selflessly working full-time for a charitable organization, then Garth Jestley's book is written for you. He has unveiled a key truth we need to embrace in this one sentence: 'When we accept our call to business, we become ambassadors for God in the secular marketplace.' Deep gratitude and thanks to Garth for inspiring the missionary in all of us."

C. Esther De Wolde, CPA, CGA
Chief Executive Officer, Phantom Screens

Published in association with The Fedd Agency, Inc., a literary agency.

Unless otherwise indicated, all Scripture quotations are taken from the Holy Bible, New Living Translation, copyright © 1996, 2004, 2015 by Tyndale House Foundation. Used by permission of Tyndale House Publishers, Carol Stream, Illinois 60188. All rights reserved.

Scripture quotations marked (MSG) are taken from THE MESSAGE, copyright © 1993, 2002, 2018 by Eugene H. Peterson. Used by permission of NavPress. Represented by Tyndale House Publishers. All rights reserved.

Scripture quotations marked (NKJV) are taken from the New King James Version®. Copyright © 1982 by Thomas Nelson. Used by permission. All rights reserved.

Scripture quotations marked (ESV) are taken from the ESV® Bible (The Holy Bible, English Standard Version®), copyright © 2001 by Crossway, a publishing ministry of Good News Publishers. Used by permission. All rights reserved.

Scripture quotations marked (KJV) are taken from the King James Version of the Bible.

Scripture quotations marked (TLB) are taken from The Living Bible copyright © 1971. Used by permission of Tyndale House Publishers, Carol Stream, Illinois 60188. All rights reserved.

Scripture quotations marked (NIV) are taken from the Holy Bible, New International Version®, NIV®. Copyright © 1973, 1978, 1984, 2011 by Biblica, Inc.™ Used by permission of Zondervan. All rights reserved worldwide. www.zondervan.com. The "NIV" and "New International Version" are trademarks registered in the United States Patent and Trademark Office by Biblica, Inc.™

ISBN: 978-1-949784-62-6
eISBN: 978-1-949784-63-3
Library of Congress Control Number: 2021904324
Printed in Canada
First Edition 21 22 23 24 / 4 3 2 1

To my wife, Mary.
This book would not have been possible if it had not been for your encouragement, editorial input, and advice—particularly in the spiritual realm. To you I owe my greatest debt of gratitude since it was your wonderful example as a passionate, fulfilled follower of Jesus that caused me to first consider His relevance to my own life. Your love for me, as well as your patient perseverance in prayer (for which I gave you lots of reasons!), culminated in my encounter with the person of Jesus in Montreal many years ago.

To our children, Skye, Mark, Erin, and Kathleen, and your families.
Thank you for your love and our many wonderful grandchildren! As you read this book, Mum and I pray you will all experience more and more of the life-giving presence of God.

CONTENTS

FOREWORD

What would you do if you won the gold medal? This was a question that came to me as I lay in bed in the wee hours of the morning in early November 1979. I was a young man, twenty-five years of age, in the terrible waiting period between writing the Uniform Final Examination (UFE) in September and the publication of the results in December. The gold medal was not for an Olympic sporting endeavor, but rather for Chartered Accountancy. It was awarded to the person in the province of British Columbia (BC) who obtained the highest mark on the UFE. My goal wasn't to get a gold medal but just to pass; if I failed, I would not be able to write the exam for another year, and my career plans would go into a holding pattern.

I hadn't studied to the extent that many of my colleagues had. My wife, Cindy, and I had moved into a new house in the spring, and Cindy had just given birth to our second son, Jeremy, about a week earlier. While many of my friends had taken several months off to study, I had given myself three weeks, which I thought would allow me adequate time to prepare for the exam.

What would you do if you won the gold medal? Somehow, I knew that it wasn't me asking myself the question, and so I responded,

Well, Lord, I didn't study enough to win the gold medal on my own, so I would have to tell everyone that You helped me. I had been raised in a Christian home and had committed my life to Christ at a young age. My worldview was different from that of many of my fellow students and colleagues, and while I often shared my faith with others, this commitment raised the bar to a whole new level. I did not hear any response from God to my answer, and I soon fell asleep, the short conversation forgotten.

A few weeks later, but still prior to receiving the exam results, one of the partners at the accounting firm at which I was articling, or interning, called me in to meet with him. I immediately thought I had somehow messed up, but I did not remember having done anything wrong. I walked into his office and was greeted with, "Please close the door, Rod, and have a seat." Okay, maybe I had screwed up.

He sat down behind his desk and said, "Rod, since I have been the Partner in Charge of this office, I have had to do a great many things that have been quite unpleasant." I was definitely in trouble—in much trouble, it appeared.

He continued. "But this is one of the better things I have had to do." He reached across the desk to shake my hand as he said, "Congratulations! You're a Chartered Accountant!"

My puzzled response was immediate. "But the results don't come out for another week."

"Rod, you won the gold medal. Congratulations!" he said as he grasped my hand and gave me a hearty handshake. "Go tell Cindy and take the rest of the day off. But don't tell anyone else. You have to keep this confidential until the results are officially posted next Friday."

In a state of shock and elation, I thanked him and headed straight to my car to drive home to tell Cindy the fantastic news (this was "BC": before cellphones). As I was driving home, a small voice spoke inside my head. It was the same internal voice that I had heard several weeks earlier at three in the morning: *Rod, you made Me a promise.*

Fear enveloped me. I wanted to go into the fetal position, but I couldn't because I was driving. The winner of the gold medal for British Columbia was also the valedictorian and was responsible for giving a speech at convocation. I had made a promise to God. I was going to stand in front of an audience of one thousand people and tell them that God had helped me.

Six weeks later, I found myself on the platform in the ballroom of the Hotel Vancouver. With me were Ken Dye, the president of the Institute of Chartered Accountants of BC (he was later to become the Auditor General of Canada), and Marcel Caron, the president of the Canadian Institute of Chartered Accountants. In front of us were all those who had passed the UFE with me, along with our families and closest friends.

I had never been so terrified in my entire life, but I had made a promise to God, and I wanted to keep it. In the middle of my five-minute speech, I said:

> We didn't arrive here on our own. We got here with the help of our family and friends, and so we thank you. You may want to thank your parents, your spouse, or your significant other. I certainly want to thank my parents and my wife, Cindy. You have been a great support to me. But most of all,

I want to thank my Lord and Savior, Jesus Christ,
for helping me get to this point in my life.

The audience clapped enthusiastically after I finished my speech. It hadn't been nearly as bad as I thought it would be. Why had I been so afraid? Relieved that it was over, I stepped down from the podium after the convocation ceremony ended. An elderly gentleman who appeared to be in his eighties stepped up to me and said, "Rod, could I have a word with you?"

We shook hands as he introduced himself. "Rod, I don't know why I am here this morning. I saw the convocation announcement and knew I had to come. Perhaps it was because I wanted to reminisce what it was like starting my career. I remember the feeling. The world was my oyster—but that was a long time ago. My wife passed away last year. I don't have much time left on this earth."

As he spoke these words, his eyes filled with tears. "But all my life, I have stood as a testimony for Jesus Christ to our profession. I can go to my grave knowing that God has put someone in my place."

The room disappeared, and I saw a relay race. One runner was carrying a baton, and as he ran, he passed it to the next runner. I looked down and saw the baton in my hands, and I heard a voice shout, "Run! RUN!"

Now we were both crying. I had experienced the culmination of another man's calling. He had passed the baton to me, and I knew what I had to do. This was my calling.

In the following years, I stood for Christ as a Chartered Accountant climbing the professional ladder, as a senior partner in one of the "Big Six" accounting firms, and later as a senior executive in Canada's second-largest private company where I reported to the owner, a man who was a perennial member of the Forbes' World's Billionaires List. While I can't say I always did an exemplary job of being a disciple of Jesus, I always knew what my calling was.

Garth Jestley joined Power to Change as the executive director of LeaderImpact in 2014, shortly after I did, and we became good friends. Like me, Garth had come from the business sector into ministry, so we had a unique bond that I did not share with many who were in ministry. He and his wife, Mary, have a passion for the gospel that is contagious, and they understand what it is to be called as Christians into the marketplace.

Some Christians in business compartmentalize the spiritual part of their lives, but I do not believe that is biblical. The psalmist tells us, *I will bless the Lord at all times; his praise shall continually be in my mouth* (Psalm 34:1, ESV).

Garth was not one who separated his career from his relationship with Jesus. As a result, he is eminently qualified to write a book on the subject of how to stand for Christ in the marketplace because he is writing from personal experience. Garth speaks in this book about being called. That is what I experienced. I was not called to be a pastor. I was called to share the love of Christ in the marketplace—to my fellow Chartered Accountants, to those I worked with, and to my clients.

The apostle Paul tells us how he adjusted to whatever culture he found himself in so he could win others to Christ. He became all things to all people that by all means he could save some (see 1 Corinthians 9:22). Paul tells us more than once that we are to imitate him (see 1 Corinthians 4:16; 11:1). We are called to share the good news of Jesus Christ with those around us. Christ's love compels Garth, me, and all who are true followers of Jesus not to live for ourselves but to live our lives for Jesus Christ (see 2 Corinthians 5:14–15).

Garth also understands the importance of apologetics in the marketplace. Apologetics is a branch of theology focused on well-reasoned arguments used to defend the Christian faith. The vast majority of Christians whom I ran into during my career were incapable of adequately defending their faith when challenged. I believe a good grasp of this important area is necessary for all Christians who want to share their faith effectively in today's culture. Garth has spent time studying apologetics, and in this book he presents information to strengthen the beliefs of the readers and to equip them with the knowledge they need in order to defend their faith with gentleness and respect.

Garth has done a commendable job of outlining what we are called to as Christians in the marketplace and how we can share our faith. He has also provided some essential tools to get you started. If you are not familiar with apologetics, I hope this will pique your interest in this vital topic. I also trust that this book will help you see your calling as a follower of Jesus to engage with those you work with and those you lead.

Rod Bergen, FCA, FCPA
President, Power to Change Ministries

PREFACE

My purpose is to give them [My followers]
a rich and satisfying life.
—JESUS (JOHN 10:10)

As a Christian leader, have you ever wondered if the rich and satisfying life promised by Jesus applies in your work life as well as in your personal and spiritual life? Have you tried to square certain aspects of business, such as profit-seeking and the drive for productivity, with Jesus' commands, or have you avoided sharing the good news of Jesus Christ because of potential negative repercussions?

Since surrendering my life to Jesus in my mid-thirties, I have met many fellow senior executives, entrepreneurs, and other leaders who have harbored similar questions. Performing at a high level, they are generally regarded as successful individuals within the culture and are committed to honoring God in their work environment. However, they don't think of their role in business as a calling from God; rather, they treat their professional career as a means to an end rather than an end in itself.

For example, many see the primary spiritual purpose of their involvement in business as a means by which to financially support the church, both locally and globally. And it doesn't help that some pastors encourage this perspective! This thinking has led many business leaders to undervalue the spiritual importance of their "day job," ascribing more value to things like short-term mission trips with their local church.

Many Christian leaders leave God at home when they go to the office, partnering with Him only when at church or when engaged in other (seemingly) more spiritual endeavors. But what if God's call on your life is in marketplace leadership?

This book explores the realities, principles, and practices of following Jesus in the marketplace based on the Bible's teaching, my own professional journey, and the counsel of other Christian leaders. While our work lives and our personal lives are both important, and maintaining proper balance between the two is critical, the primary focus of this book is the professional side of our lives.

I pray you will be greatly encouraged in your role as a marketplace leader. It is a legitimate and deeply fulfilling calling. Because of your influence within this very important sphere, you are uniquely qualified to make an outsized impact for the kingdom of God.

You are much more than your business card.

Introduction

CALLED TO PASSION

Is this it? This question popped into my head moments after receiving a note from Bill Spencer, then president of Citibank New York, congratulating me on my appointment as a vice president of the bank. It was the 1970s, and the promotion wasn't just significant to me because of my relative youth and the authority that the role provided, but it was also the realization of a personal goal I had established three years earlier. However, the elation I had from achieving my goal quickly dissipated. The promotion seemed somehow anticlimactic.

In pursuit of advancement, I had put my family through a lot of disruption, including three big interprovincial and international moves over a short time frame. In some cases, we did not even get around to unpacking boxes before we moved again. Yet after all the sacrifice, I suddenly found myself questioning the meaning behind the corporate race I had been running. That great sense of fulfillment I anticipated upon reaching this milestone eluded me. Instead, I was left with a sense of discouragement. That evening, I tried to recapture that celebratory feeling with a few drinks.

Up to that point, I would have characterized my life, both professional and personal, as successful and fulfilling. I had always outperformed, both academically and professionally. My personal life was also fulfilling, thanks to my wonderful wife, Mary, and our two (now four) wonderful children. My life's trajectory was seemingly a continuous sequence of positive milestones that always brought satisfaction, but I suddenly found myself wondering whether I was missing the deeper meaning behind everything in my life.

About a year prior to our first move with Citibank from Toronto to Montreal, Mary had a dramatic encounter with the person of Jesus Christ that deeply satisfied her search for fulfillment. Shortly after this encounter, she shared her experience with me one evening during dinner. I was momentarily stunned. Gathering my wits, I said something to the effect of "Does this mean you're going to stand on a corner in downtown Toronto and hand out Bibles?"

My (admittedly crude) response might have seemed sarcastic, but it was really just my shocked reaction to the genuine change I saw in Mary. She positively exuded the fulfillment she was experiencing. Jesus had become incredibly real for her, and the powerful change in her demeanor was obvious. Over the following weeks, she exhibited a new joy, peace, excitement, and confidence as she studied her Bible and attended a nearby church.

While pleased for Mary, I regarded her decision as having no direct relevance to my own life. I was both satisfied in, and absorbed by, my race to the top. I believed that religion was irrelevant to my business career. I largely defined life in terms of a continuous process of setting and exceeding career goals, thereby earning raises, bonuses, and promotions. Since this process was, at the time, satisfying to me, I felt no need to step back and reassess my life.

Yet when I learned of my promotion at Citibank, the goal I had been working so hard to reach, I experienced a startling feeling of emptiness. Regardless, I put on a brave front and didn't share my inner struggle with anyone. However, privately I became more and more preoccupied with the true meaning of life.

A few months later, I accepted yet another promotion as Citibank's Head of Corporate Banking for Eastern Canada, based in Montreal. A little more than a year after the family joined me in Montreal, two major Canadian banks approached me concurrently with attractive executive offers. Perhaps it was the "grass is always greener on the other side of the fence" syndrome, but the offers had a certain appeal. Late in the year, I accepted an offer from one of the banks and made plans to move back to Toronto early the next year.

The excitement of career advancement notwithstanding, I remained unfulfilled in the deepest sense and was open to new ideas. Shortly before Christmas and just prior to our move back to Toronto, Mary asked if I would like to join her and the children at church that day. In light of my growing receptivity to exploring the question of meaning, I accepted her invitation. However, I was dubious about the benefits, and I said so. Mary had no problem with my skepticism, and off we went.

That day, the young assistant pastor at the neighborhood church began his sermon with a challenge. After listing several possible reasons for attending church, including, for example, to demonstrate moral virtue, he suggested that none of them would win God's favor. He then encouraged anyone who was attending primarily for said reasons to consider leaving. Immediately, some folks in the pews got up and left! Until then, I had held the (largely uninformed) view that many, if not most, Christians were more concerned with appearing holier than others, yet here was this pastor calling them out! His credibility in my estimation shot up. He had my full attention.

The following Sunday, Mary had no difficulty persuading me to join her at church. After the opening prayers and hymns, the senior pastor got up to speak. At some point during his message, I distinctly heard the words, "I am alive," and they were not coming from the pulpit! In an instant, I knew with certainty that the speaker was Jesus and that those three little words were absolutely true. Experiencing the reality of God's presence, I was overwhelmed. Moreover, it seemed obvious to me that since Jesus was alive, He was God. So logically (and we mathematicians love logic!), that would mean that God Himself wanted a personal relationship with me! In the moment, it was truly the offer I couldn't refuse! I decided on the spot to obey Him in whatever He wanted me to do.

Prior to that day, my knowledge of the Christian worldview didn't go much beyond having heard a few Bible verses as I was growing up. But in that moment, I became absolutely certain that God existed and that He wanted a relationship with me right then, just as I was. It was as though a switch had been pulled inside me, and I was a completely different person. Subsequently, when I read the following excerpt from the apostle Paul's letter to the church at Corinth, I understood what had happened to me: *This means that anyone who belongs to Christ has become a new person. The old life is gone; a new life has begun!* (2 Corinthians 5:17).

It is no exaggeration to say that everything changed. In the days after, I experienced a continual awareness of God's presence wherever I was.

Although I didn't yet understand where this newfound faith in God was taking me, I did know with certainty that I was destined to spend eternity with Him. C. S. Lewis, Christian author and former atheist, put it this way: "If we find ourselves with a desire that nothing in this world can satisfy, the most probable explanation is that we were made for another world."[1]

I discovered a unique intimacy with God that cannot be found in any other relationship, even in a strong marriage. I began to wonder whether He wanted me to make a wholesale life change. How could He possibly want me to continue in the corporate world? Should I not be doing something more spiritual? After wrestling with these questions, however, my family decided to move back to Toronto, so I could take up my new position with the bank.

Other aspects of my life changed in short order. Up to that time, I was drinking a lot. I think it was one of my ways of dealing with dissatisfaction. When I turned my life over to God, though, the desire for alcohol completely left me, and it was years before I felt the liberty to enjoy any alcoholic beverages (and then not in excess). In addition, my attitude toward money changed immediately. For some reason, fear of financial lack had previously resulted in a tight-fisted attitude when it came to generosity. While the fear was slow to leave, I experienced a radically new desire to give, and Mary and I began a journey of generosity that has continued to this day.

Life from that point on was not always smooth sailing, but I experienced an unexplainable peace through various storms, including business reversals and cancer. The principal reason was because, to this day, I have never lost the very real sense of God's intimate presence,

1. C. S. Lewis, *Mere Christianity* (New York: Macmillan, 1960).

whether in leadership at the bank or as CEO and shareholder of a Toronto-based private investment management company, although I still wrestled with the relevance of faith in God in the workplace. The reality is that Christian marketplace leaders will always face pressure to conform to the views and behaviors of those around them. However, Jesus commands us to seek the kingdom of God above all else—even in the workplace. In this way, we differentiate ourselves and influence those around us to consider the relevance of faith in God in respect to their own lives.

Early in my relationship with God, I experienced a tension between my identity as a follower of Jesus and the identity proclaimed by my business card. It seemed I was faced with choosing between the two. I learned that it is God, not my company, who determines my identity. He called me to leadership in the business realm and gave me various gifts in order to reach people who may not otherwise hear the gospel. In today's world, marketplace leaders are a widely overlooked and unreached people group.[2]

Throughout my years in the corporate world, I have wrestled with several questions related to living out my faith in that realm. The first relates to business as a calling. Was I meant to follow Jesus into my workplace, particularly in light of all the cultural obstacles? Why is it important to Jesus that I treat my business life as a calling? What would I need to know to be effective in this calling? What does business as a calling actually look like?

These questions led me to explore the meaning of a calling, the implications of the Great Commandment and the Great Commission

2. Years ago, Mary and I defined our life purpose as "to know Jesus better and to better make Him known." This purpose statement applies not only to the personal side of life but also to the professional side.

regarding my attitudes and conduct in the workplace, the centrality of an intimate relationship with Jesus, and the importance of being armed with confident responses to skeptics' objections. Equipped with complete answers to these questions, we become effective and fruitful ambassadors for Jesus in the marketplace.

Be open to the possibility that you are in exactly the place God wants you to be in order to fulfill His specific plans and purposes in creating you. As you wake up to the reality that God has called you to leadership in business or some other realm, you will experience greater fulfillment than ever before.

†

Part 1:
CALLED TO BUSINESS

CAN I FOLLOW JESUS IN THE MARKETPLACE?

Chapter 1

IS BUSINESS A REAL CALLING, AND IF SO, IS IT AN IMPORTANT ONE?

As a prisoner for the Lord, then, I urge you to live
a life worthy of the calling you have received.

—THE APOSTLE PAUL (EPHESIANS 4:1)

How many leaders do you know who proudly declare they are called to business? For most of us, the answer is very few, if any. There is often ambivalence among Christians toward the concept of business as a legitimate calling.[3] Alternatively, some people might acknowledge its legitimacy while questioning its importance or spiritual significance relative to other occupations. That ambivalence toward business is not limited to followers of Jesus.

---

3. Throughout this book, the words "marketplace" and "business" will be used interchangeably. Business is a part of, though not all of, the marketplace. The marketplace is defined herein as the world outside the Christian church, which is the body of all believers everywhere (see Ephesians 1:22–23). Therefore, marketplace leaders include not only business leaders but also leaders in every realm of human endeavor, including government, education, the arts and the media, the military, and the judiciary, as well as the legal, medical, and other so-called "professions." This definition explicitly excludes those called to vocational ministry within a local church setting.

I remember an incident during my junior high school years in Vancouver, Canada. On one occasion, my guidance counselor asserted that we were in real trouble if we didn't know what we were going to do with the rest of our lives. Since the average age of the students in our class was thirteen, it was a curious, if not dubious, proposition!

In a state of near panic that evening, I consulted my father, for whom I had great respect and admiration. A successful lawyer, he favored a career in that field but allowed that I might also consider other "worthy" professions such as medicine, engineering, accounting, and architecture. He even mentioned Christian ministry, although I wasn't paying attention to Jesus at the time. In his view, these professions represented the most noble of my vocational options. Notably absent from this list was a career in business, even though he specialized in corporate law!

While I liked and excelled at every subject in school, I particularly enjoyed the study of biology. Without further consideration, I chose medicine, and in doing so, got the guidance counselor off my back. That onetime decision carried me all the way through high school and undergraduate studies at the University of British Columbia. In the course of earning a Bachelor of Science degree with a major in mathematics, I completed the pre-med curriculum, after which I took the medical entrance exams. Only then did I confront the reality that I could not even stomach the sight of blood—and so my promising medical career ended before it started. Obviously, I should have given more thought to this problematic detail prior to deciding on a career in medicine!

One positive outcome of this seemingly futile experience was that I met Mary, my wife, in Physiology 201. Introduced by a mutual friend, Mary was taking the course in pursuit of a Bachelor of Science degree in rehabilitation medicine. She graduated two years later, one year after me, and then we got married in Vancouver.

Before Mary and I got married, I had to establish an alternative career direction since medicine was no longer an option for me. Since I was not following Jesus at the time, I turned to my friends for advice. They recommended I earn an MBA since I excelled at math and business involved a lot of math. I followed their advice and was accepted at the Business School at the University of Western Ontario (now the Ivey Business School at Western University) where I began laying the foundation for my career in business.

Though I enjoyed and excelled in the business field, my father's perspective on the hierarchy of career fields is not uncommon. From a Christian perspective, business doesn't immediately stand out as a high-value contributor either to the common good or to building the kingdom of God. Those of us pursuing business often find ourselves asking if we can actually honor God in business, or even if business is, in some way, tainted. Based on much reflection and experience, however, I would argue that not only is business a legitimate and important calling, but it is also not unlike other professions, including vocational ministry. While there are some elephants in the room in regard to the intrinsic moral virtue of the field, let's first focus on the issue of business as a calling.

From the moment I first encountered Jesus when I was in my mid-thirties, I knew everything had changed because my identity had changed (see 2 Corinthians 5:17). In fact, given the vividness of this encounter, I momentarily questioned whether it was possible to remain in the corporate world. Jesus was so real to me that I simply wanted to share my experience of this new life with everyone I met. It seemed inconceivable that I could fulfill this passion in any way other than vocational ministry. Can you relate?

Fueled by my deep desire to do whatever God wanted me to do, Mary and I even briefly considered moving to a developing nation to tell people about Jesus. This is a not uncommon response when people surrender their lives to Jesus. Motivated by a life-changing encounter with Jesus, we can easily find ourselves thinking that vocational ministry is not only the most important calling for a believer, but that it is also the most approved in Jesus' eyes. Basically, we conclude that callings fall into a spiritual hierarchy, with vocational ministry (including working in parachurch organizations) at the apex.

However, this view does not agree with the Bible's perspective. According to the apostle Peter, all believers are on the same spiritual plane (see 1 Peter 2:9). Regardless of one's chosen field of endeavor, we are all equal in the sense that we are made in God's image and are reconciled to Him based upon our response to Jesus' sacrificial death on the cross and not upon our own good deeds. What matters is how we obey God's leading when pursuing His call on our lives, not to what vocation we are called.

In fact, the apostle Paul provides the following guidance for new believers: *Each of you, dear brothers and sisters, should remain as you were when God first called you* (1 Corinthians 7:24). God's call on each of us is activated when we receive Jesus' offer of forgiveness and surrender our will to His. By extension, Paul is saying we should stay where we are when we make Jesus Lord, unless, of course, we are involved in some sort of morally questionable activity. Paul's exhortation makes good sense. After all, the change our co-workers observe in our attitude and conduct can really impact them and cause them to ask questions about their own lives. That noticeable change makes us particularly effective in reaching others in our spheres of influence with the gospel.

After praying with Mary about the decision, I decided to remain in the corporate world. However, it was no longer business as usual. My life was not my own since Jesus had bought and paid for it. As a result, I was not free to follow my own passions and desires without reference to Him and His will for my life. Discerning God's will is sometimes elusive. After all, He doesn't typically instruct us via an audible voice! He does, however, communicate continually to every believer through the inner witness of the Holy Spirit. This leading must not conflict with Scripture, which declares itself to be the inspired word of God (see 2 Timothy 3:16). For me, praying with (and learning from) Mary and meeting in community with others who have a genuine relationship with God through Jesus have been key to my discerning the leading of the Holy Spirit.

Over the years, I have learned more about the subject of callings. *Calling* means "a strong urge towards a particular way of life or career; a vocation."[4] The Merriam-Webster dictionary adds a spiritual dimension: "a strong inner impulse toward a particular course of action especially when accompanied by conviction of divine influence."[5]

A calling implies a caller. Obviously, you do not call yourself! I think Merriam-Webster's definition is truer to the historical usage of

4. "Calling." Lexico Dictionaries | English. Oxford English Dictionary. Accessed March 2, 2021. https://www.lexico.com/en/definition/calling.
5. "Calling." Merriam-Webster. Accessed March 2, 2021. https://www.merriam-webster.com/dictionary/calling.

the word than Oxford's purely secular take. In the world of those who profess to follow Jesus, a calling implies responding to Jesus' call when He says, "Follow Me." This response to Jesus implies following His example and obeying His commands in every venue of life.

The writings of the early church leaders, especially the apostle Paul, explore every facet of a Christian's identity as a child of God, and one of the predominant themes is *calling*. There are eighty-seven references to calling (or being called) in the various letters to the early church. According to the Bible, I am called to be an ambassador for Jesus in the marketplace (see 2 Corinthians 5:20). That is, I am called to represent Jesus' perspective in every aspect of business to the best of my ability.

Actually, the apostle Paul himself was engaged in marketplace ministry. After his initial encounter with Jesus on the road to Damascus, he received his assignment: proclaim Jesus' name to the gentiles, to their kings, and to the people of Israel (see Acts 9:15). Two aspects of this call are particularly relevant to reaching business leaders. First, Paul was commanded to share the good news with kings. In light of their significant authority and influence, business leaders can reasonably be viewed as royalty in our time. Second, like business leaders, kings primarily fulfill their role in the marketplace (i.e., not in places of worship). To reach them with the gospel, Paul had to pursue them on their home turf. He pursued his calling while at the same time plying his own trade as a tentmaker (see Acts 18:3). In going to the people, Paul followed the example of Jesus, who did most of His ministry outside the synagogues and temple precincts.

Andrew Wommack, a teacher and prolific author, provides a useful perspective on *calling* to which I wholeheartedly subscribe. He writes, "God is not asking us to live for Him [in the marketplace]. He is asking us to let Him live through us [in the marketplace] (Galatians 2:20). The Christian life is not a changed life but an exchanged life. This can only be accomplished when the Holy Spirit is leading and empowering us."[6] Of course, like others in ambassadorial roles, I sometimes fail to accurately represent my boss! The good news is that God has already forgiven my shortcomings and consistently provides the necessary grace to help me get back on my feet.

The best way I know to describe my call to business is to say that every day is another opportunity to live out my relationship with Jesus in the marketplace. This means I am in regular communion with Him throughout the business day, particularly in challenging business situations, which include both negative and positive developments. Successes can often become greater challenges to our Christian witness than failures.

While exploring the subject of callings over the years, I have been greatly influenced by the time I have been able to spend with the author and Christian thought leader Os Guinness. He maintains that all followers of Jesus have the same primary calling, which is to know God, know His Word, and share the good news of salvation through Jesus Christ. In addition, each Christian has a secondary calling that flows from God's leading and their unique makeup, which involves their societal position, gifts, and passions. While the secondary calling is very important, it is subordinate to the primary calling. Therefore, if we aren't being true to our primary calling in whatever we choose to do, we aren't really fulfilling our calling![7]

6. Andrew Wommack, "The Power to Serve." iDisciple.Org. Andrew Wommack Ministries International, February 6, 2021. https://www.idisciple.org/post/the-power-to-serve.
7. On occasion, I have provoked some pastor friends by suggesting that we both have the same primary calling. However, their secondary calling is pastoring, while mine is business!

From the foregoing line of argument, business is clearly a legitimate secondary calling, but is it an important one? Based upon conversations I have had over the years, I have concluded that many Christians and non-Christians today simply don't understand the central and constructive role this realm plays in their own lives and in the lives of their families, their communities, their nations, and the entire world.

For purposes of this discussion, the business domain is defined as comprising all commercial activity of private sector enterprises engaged in the provision of goods and services to satisfy market demand. It excludes activities of public sector entities that deliver services to the public, including education, healthcare, public safety, and transportation.

Based upon empirical data, the free enterprise system, of which private sector businesses are the linchpin, is critical to healthy economies and human flourishing. By contrast, collective ownership schemes like communism have consistently failed to deliver their utopian promises, sometimes spectacularly.

Three factors underpin the importance of the business sector. First, private sector businesses are the creative engine of any healthy economy. Second, commercial activity is directly and indirectly the source of funding for everything within the economy. Third, the influence of business in any society is substantial and pervasive. From a Christian perspective, engagement in business generally and business leadership specifically provides anyone called to this arena with significant opportunities for creativity, contribution, and influence. Let's dive a little deeper into these three ideas.

BUSINESSES ARE ENGINES OF CREATIVITY

Creativity is "the ability to produce or use original and unusual ideas."[8] The ultimate source of all creativity is God. He authored everything in the beginning when He spoke the heavens and the earth into existence. The more that science uncovers the complexity and fine-tuning of the cosmos, the more humanity is faced with evidence of an immeasurably great power behind creation. But God didn't just create the realms of space, time, energy, and matter. He also created humanity in His image, meaning we not only have free will, but also we are designed to emulate His creativity in our own lives.

The term *creativity* is usually reserved for the world of artistic expression. However, it is not the sole realm of creativity. Taken as a whole, the business sector is enormously creative. Simply consider the amount of human progress since 1900.[9] In particular, the magnitude of technological advancement is difficult to grasp. No doubt someone living in 1900 would have regarded predictions of a world like that of the twenty-first century as pure science fiction! As a result of advances in many different fields, such as agronomy, construction, transportation, communications, finance, and medicine, humanity has flourished.

Most of that progress can be attributed to private sector businesses that, in the pursuit of profit, strive to meet the needs of people. As will

8. "Creativity." Cambridge English Dictionary. Accessed March 2, 2021. https://dictionary.cambridge.org/us/dictionary/english/creativity.

9. Of course, "progress" is not uniform across the globe, nor is it all positive. For example, an argument can be made that there has been absolutely no moral progress over the last several centuries. We only need to consider the huge ideologically driven wars of the twentieth century. Also, it is undeniable that technology has played a major role in harming people as well as helping them.

be discussed in the next chapter, profit-seeking is not evil. Rather, it is an absolutely essential ingredient in any well-functioning economic system. It provides the necessary motivation for risk-taking, and it results in the most effective (though imperfect) allocation of capital among business enterprises based upon prospective risk-adjusted returns on investment.

Of course, creativity goes hand in glove with the possibility of failure or risk. One might argue that risk capital chases creativity. In order to prosper over the long term, businesses must not only sell quality products and services but must also price them attractively and deliver them cost effectively. If any one of these three critical success factors is lacking, businesses become unsustainable over time and ultimately fail. Successful businesses sustain themselves by producing and using original and unusual ideas. Obvious examples include technology giants such as Microsoft, Apple, Google, and Amazon. Clearly, the ability to innovate plays a central role in their enormous growth and profitability. However, creativity is not the sole preserve of technology giants.

Every business, from the very small to the very large, functions creatively as it strives to satisfy market demand. Consider the investment management business I led for many years. The company's overarching purpose is to create innovative investment products that help investors achieve their financial objectives. On an ongoing basis, the company launches new funds that have never existed before. Even if there are similar funds sponsored by the company or its competitors, every fund is different in terms of its investment thesis and the execution of its investment strategy. Besides fund design, other creative elements include marketing strategy and ongoing investment management after the fund has been created.

Risk is ever present for the simple reason that success depends not only on the merit of the investment thesis and favorable market conditions but also on the fund finding favor with many different stakeholders. While the investment business differs from other industries, all must innovate. If they don't, they ultimately fail.

For a follower of Jesus and a marketplace leader, business is not just a creative outlet, but it is also a place where the believer has a unique advantage. In the apostle Paul's second letter to the fledgling church in Corinth, he challenges them with the question, *Do you not know yourselves, that Jesus Christ is in you?* (2 Corinthians 13:5 NKJV).

This question is rhetorical. According to the Bible, believers are indwelt by the Spirit of Christ. Since God is the author of creativity, Christian leaders can look to Him for creative ideas, and since He knows everything, this is a profound asset when leading an organization to creatively accomplish its unique mission.

BUSINESSES ARE ENGINES OF FUNDING

In 2020, I spent considerable time sheltering in place in the midst of the COVID-19 pandemic. Economies around the world were shut down by government edicts aimed at bringing the pandemic under control. While there was considerable debate as to when and how businesses should be permitted to operate, there was no serious argument concerning the necessity of allowing businesses to begin normal functioning again. If they didn't begin to function normally again, countries around the world could suffer enormous long-term harm at the expense of their economies.

To bridge to the time when the private sector can operate with a modicum of normalcy, governments collectively injected trillions of dollars of liquidity into their economies through massive monetary stimulus and unprecedented fiscal measures. The goal of these actions is to support the workers adversely affected by shutdown orders and the businesses that employ them. Many seem oblivious to the simple truth that private sector for-profit business funds everything. And by everything, I mean absolutely everything. It is unfortunate that it took a pandemic and the governmental response to affirm this fundamental truth. In fact, private sector for-profit businesses fund not only private sector activities but all government and not-for-profit services.

Whether we are talking about healthcare, education, public transportation, the arts, the police, other emergency services, or any of the myriad not-for-profit organizations, the ultimate source of funding for every one of these worthwhile endeavors is private sector for-profit businesses. It is true that individuals are a significant funding source for governments and the not-for-profit sector; however, these individuals earn the money with which to pay taxes, make donations from paychecks, or earn dividends and interest from either private sector businesses or the various non-business entities funded directly or indirectly by business.

While all cultural arenas, including education, medicine, the arts, the media, religious organizations, and government, are important to human flourishing, it is only commercial activity that ultimately provides the necessary funding that enables them to operate and thrive.

BUSINESSES ARE ENGINES OF INFLUENCE

At the invitation of a close friend several years ago, Mary and I attended the National Prayer Breakfast in Washington, DC. For many years, our friend has played a leadership role in a group of business executives and other professionals who meet annually in conjunction with the prayer breakfast. Their purpose is to network and hear from other leaders on issues pertaining to faith in God in their professional and personal lives.

On this occasion, Pastor Rick Warren joined our group and shared the following story. A CEO of a large multinational corporation that employed tens of thousands of people around the world once called him to request a meeting. The CEO explained he had become a follower of Jesus as a result of reading Warren's *Purpose Driven Life* book. Warren agreed to meet.

The major question on the CEO's mind was whether God was calling him into vocational ministry (the same kind of thoughts I had after encountering Jesus). While it is conceivable that this executive might have become a very influential pastor someday, Warren's view was that his highest and best use was to remain where he was until God called him elsewhere. When we consider our place in the kingdom of God and where we can most effectively share the gospel, the primary question to be answered isn't what job is more worthy, but rather, what is God calling us to do now?

The CEO in Warren's story had significant influence over the lives of each person who reported directly to him, who in turn were people of enormous influence. The CEO's influence did not just impact the executives reporting to him but also indirectly impacted the lives of the thousands of employees who were led by each executive. In short, marketplace leaders are people of enormous influence either for good or evil. The fact that we occupy these influential positions is actually a gift from God. Through these positions of responsibility, we can glorify Him by fulfilling His plans and purposes in our professional lives.

LeaderImpact, the organization I was privileged to lead, is premised on the power of influence. In the twenty-first century, most leaders are unlikely to darken the door of a church of their own accord. This reality has several explanations. Some leaders don't see the relevance of faith in God to the real world in which they operate. For others, their lives, however imperfect, just work for them and they don't feel a need to address the bigger questions like ultimate purpose and destiny. Finally, some people cannot relate to people in other fields.

For this reason, the LeaderImpact platform is built on small professional peer groups. At the invitation of their professional colleagues, many non-believers around the world are prepared to explore these issues within these groups. Why? Simply because they are more receptive to the relevance of faith in God in their own lives when they see its relevance in the lives of their peers.

I would like to share about my friend Oscar. He is an excellent example of someone who pursued business as a calling. While Mary and I had known Oscar and his family for many years through our local church, we had failed to see and appreciate his profound impact within his workplace. At his funeral following his untimely death from a heart attack at age fifty-one, one of his co-workers delivered a deeply moving eulogy. Here is a representative sampling of comments about Oscar from many different co-workers from every level of the large organization at which he worked:

- He was always joyful.
- He made our day brighter.
- He was always encouraging.
- He never complained.
- He was an excellent member of the finance team.
- I will miss conversations about God.

The CEO of the company for which Oscar had worked was unable to attend the funeral, but she shared about Oscar's significant and positive impact on the entire work community. An influencer of influencers, Oscar responded to God's call and made a lasting impact in his unique sphere of influence, both professionally and spiritually.

WAKE-UP CALL

Can you tell anyone you meet that you are called to business? As you approach each business day, are you excited by what the Lord has in store for you? After all, He has called you to be there. According to the New Testament, the One for whom nothing is impossible indwells you by His Holy Spirit!

When you learn to adopt this mindset, problems become opportunities to glorify God. Likewise, every time you engage with someone—including your staff, members of your board, customers, and suppliers—becomes an opportunity to honor God. In other words, as my friend Oscar exemplified, each day at work becomes a faith adventure.

Here is a thought experiment. Imagine that someone asks you why you decided on business as your career choice. My answer is,

"Initially, I got into business because it played to my interests and strengths and offered tremendous personal and financial benefits. After I became a follower of Jesus, I remained in business because He has called me to follow Him in the marketplace." What is your answer?

By responding to the question in this way, you are setting the table for a deeper conversation. If not immediately, it could be sometime down the road. By the way, you can set up this sort of encounter by asking other people why they chose business. There is a real possibility that they will turn around and ask you the same question. If not, you can ask their permission to share your reason for being in business.

My prayer is that an army of marketplace leaders will passionately answer Jesus' call to the marketplace—not only becoming confident in their calling to business, but openly declaring it. Visualize for a moment an army of Christian business leaders marching under the banner of "Called to Business." Given the huge influence of business leaders, such an army would have the potential to turn the world upside down!

Chapter 2

WOULD THE ELEPHANT IN THE ROOM PLEASE STAND UP?

*I am going to argue that many aspects of
business activity are morally good in themselves,
and that in themselves they bring glory to God—
though they also have great potential for
misuse and wrongdoing.*

—DR. WAYNE GRUDEM, *BUSINESS FOR THE GLORY OF GOD*

Many individuals have ambivalent feelings toward a career in business. The elephant in the room is the (usually unspoken) assumption that business is morally neutral at best, if not downright evil. Free-market capitalism has been subjected to a concerted assault from proponents of Critical Theory, a complex and multifaceted field of study that has emerged over the last several decades. It has permeated the academy and has seeped into the church, even influencing some church leaders who generally espouse biblical orthodoxy. Additionally, many young people have unknowingly absorbed its claims without thinking through all its logical entailments.

This negative mindset often affects the Christians' willingness to consider business as a legitimate calling or to enthusiastically embrace it. Consequently, many Christians fall into the trap of seeing business as simply a means to an end or a placeholder until, as discussed in the previous chapter, a more spiritual calling materializes. But what if Grudem's foregoing assertion is correct?[10]

What if business can possess an intrinsic moral goodness that provides many and varied opportunities to glorify God? After all, according to the Westminster Shorter Catechism, "man's chief end is to glorify God." By extension, the pursuit of a career in business becomes a legitimate candidate for calling. The following questions address several issues of importance, not only to believers but to society as a whole.

IS OWNERSHIP MORALLY GOOD?

Having lived in advanced Western economies my entire life, I have never once questioned the moral goodness of ownership. I have taken it for granted and have happily exercised my right to own assets. In

10. According to *Encyclopaedia Britannica*, "Critical Theory is a Marxist-inspired movement in social and political philosophy originally associated with the work of the Frankfurt School. Drawing particularly on the thought of Karl Marx and Sigmund Freud, critical theorists maintain that a primary goal of philosophy is to understand and to help overcome the social structures through which people are dominated and oppressed. Believing that science, like other forms of knowledge, has been used as an instrument of oppression, they caution against a blind faith in scientific progress, arguing that scientific knowledge must not be pursued as an end in itself without reference to the goal of human emancipation. Since the 1970s, critical theory has been immensely influential in the study of history, law, literature, and the social sciences." "Critical Theory." Encyclopædia Britannica. Accessed March 2, 2021. https://www.britannica.com/topic/critical-theory.

fact, by encouraging risk-taking, ownership is the backbone of any market economy. For example, I wouldn't have bought an ownership interest in my business without the potential rewards of dividends and capital appreciation. My risk-taking paid off, though not without a few speed bumps along the way!

However, it is becoming more popular in Western culture to advocate for socialism or collective ownership of the means of production. Given the consistent historical failure of socialism to create vibrant economies that benefit the populace as a whole, it is alarming that many people continue to flirt with the idea.[11] People often seem enamored with the thinking of academics like Noam Chomsky, who has said, "A consistent anarchist must oppose private ownership of the means of production, and the wage-slavery which is a component of this system, as incompatible with the principle that labor must be freely undertaken and under the control of the producer."[12] Influenced by this idea, some Christians today are ambivalent to the concept of private ownership.

According to the Bible, we are made in the image of God (see Genesis 1:27) and are called to imitate Him (see Ephesians 5:1–2). Regarding imitation, in *Business for the Glory of God,* Grudem says:

> Ownership of possessions is a fundamental way
> that we imitate God's sovereignty over the universe

11. See the article "CNN thinks that socialism is cool. My grandparents from the USSR would disagree" by Alex Berezow, a PhD microbiologist and Senior Fellow of Biomedical Science at the American Council on Science and Health, and a member of *USA Today's* Board of Contributors. https://www.usatoday.com/story/opinion/2018/02/21/cnn-thinks-socialism-cool-my-grandparents-ussr-would-disagree/349830002/.
12. Alison Edgley, *In Social and Political Thought of Noam Chomsky.* (Hoboken: Taylor and Francis, 2013), 50.

by our exercising "sovereignty" over a tiny portion of the universe, the things we own. When we take care of our possessions, we imitate God in His taking care of the whole universe, and He delights to see us imitate Him in this way. In addition, when we care for our possessions, it gives us opportunity to imitate many other attributes of God, such as wisdom, knowledge, beauty, creativity, love for others, kindness, fairness, independence, freedom, exercise of will, blessedness (or joy), and so forth.[13]

As Creator, God owns everything, including us (see Psalm 24:1). Followers of Jesus are actually stewards of the assets with which He has entrusted us. Besides meeting our material needs, ownership of the assets entrusted to us empowers us to give to others. Imitating God's generosity to the best of our ability calls for us to give not only of our time and talents but also of our material resources. God commands, not suggests, that we should be generous. While abuses of ownership are sadly all too common, that reality does not negate the intrinsic moral goodness of ownership intended by God. As followers of Jesus in the marketplace, however, we look to Him for guidance regarding the use of the resources He has entrusted to us.

ARE PROFITS AND PROFIT-SEEKING MORALLY GOOD?

Growing up in the sixties amid the hippy generation, I was exposed to

13. Wayne A. Grudem, *Business for the Glory of God* (Wheaton: Crossway Books, 2003), 19-20.

lots of antipathy toward the corporate world, including profit-seeking. Many of my contemporaries were anti-establishment and viewed profits as emblematic of greed. Even well-known Christian author Philip Yancey has said, "People instinctively know the difference between something done with a profit motive and something done with a love motive."[14]

As a strong free-market advocate before and after my initial encounter with Jesus, I have never understood questions concerning the intrinsic goodness of profits. Of course, there will always be opportunities in business for unjust enrichment through unethical behavior that is motivated by profit-seeking. Wearing my investor hat, however, I wouldn't consider investing in a business I didn't believe could generate a profit commensurate with its risk profile. With due respect to Philip Yancey, whom I admire as a writer and who is a follower of Jesus, the profit motive and the love motive do not have to be mutually exclusive. If I were to transfer all the return my shareholders earned through risk-taking either to customers by selling products at cost or raising the wages of my employees, that would betray the trust of my investors. Moreover, the lack of profitability would eventually shutter the business, resulting in loss to all stakeholders, including customers and employees.

As followers of Jesus, we must turn to the Bible to determine God's perspective on profit. As it happens, Jesus addressed the morality of profits and profit-seeking. While some have taken this particular teaching of Jesus to be a metaphorical reference to the talents with which God has endowed us, there is no reason to conclude that

14. Philip Yancey, "Philip Yancey Quote." Citatis.com. Accessed March 18, 2021. https://citatis.com/a14380/1fac5/.

it doesn't also apply to financial stewardship. Sitting with His disciples on the Mount of Olives, Jesus tells the story of a man who, prior to going on a journey, entrusted his wealth to three servants (see Matthew 25:14–30). To one he gave five units of money, to another he gave two, and to another he gave one.

Upon his return after a long journey, he commended the first two servants for doubling the wealth entrusted to them. When the third confessed that he had simply buried the money, the wealthy man called him wicked and lazy and ordered the transfer of his money to the first servant! In essence, Jesus defined profit and seeking profit as morally good, and He defined not seeking profit as wicked. Of course, this philosophy does not apply to not-for-profit organizations for which the good works they perform are the return on donors' investments.

Again, it must be emphasized that sometimes businesses, in the pursuit of profit, conduct themselves in ways that are not illegal but are morally questionable. This reality does not, however, invalidate the constructive and essential role of profit-seeking.

IS THE DRIVE TO BE MORE PRODUCTIVE MORALLY GOOD?

As I consider my material blessings, I am grateful that God created humankind with a drive to be productive. According to the Bible, we are made in God's image (see Genesis 1:27) and are called to imitate Him (see Ephesians 5:1–2). By creating the entire universe (both living and non-living), God demonstrates the concept of productivity beyond human comprehension.

Every material object I possess, including my house, car, computer, phone, clean running water, and everything else, is the end result of human productivity. By exploring the creation, gaining knowledge, and applying wisdom, people have discovered and invented innumerable ways to derive useful products from the earth's vast resources. In doing so, they facilitate human flourishing. Technological advances are the direct result of the increased output of useful products or services per worker.

How does output per worker increase? First, as individuals, we can work smarter and harder. The Bible says, *Whoever is slack in his work is a brother to him who destroys* (Proverbs 18:9, ESV). In his letter to the church at Colossae, the apostle Paul says, *Don't just do the minimum that will get you by. Do your best. Work from the heart for your real Master, for God, confident that you'll get paid in full when you come into your inheritance. . . . The sullen servant who does shoddy work will be held responsible. Being Christian doesn't cover up bad work* (Colossians 3:22–25, MSG).

Second, marketplace leaders can assign roles and organize the activities of employees in such a way that the enterprise becomes more efficient and more effective. As a result, the cost of production declines and, in competitive markets, ultimately drives down the price of goods and services. Finally, new technologies enable individuals and organizations to be more productive.

Some see the drive for productivity as immoral in the sense that more production is squeezed out of fewer people. While there are certainly companies that exploit their workforce, most people enjoy being more productive. Laziness does not excuse poor productivity. Poor productivity endangers the health of the entire enterprise since high-cost producers ultimately fail, and when they do, the needs of others are not met. These others include buyers of their goods, suppliers, people who want to work, banks, and shareholders.

IS COMPETITION MORALLY GOOD?

Most of the people I have dealt with in the marketplace are highly competitive. I certainly am. For example, I remember the thrill of beating out other major international banks to lead a large financing of a new aluminum smelter. In the trade, we call these competitions "beauty contests"—because to beat these global competitors, we are compelled to bring all our skills to bear. The very presence of such reputable and powerful competitors caused us to put our best foot forward. Alternatively, as a buyer of investment banking services over the years, my firm held our own beauty contests to determine which banks would lead the initial public offerings for the new funds we had created.

How is it, then, that some see competition as a dirty word? The expression "dog eat dog" comes to mind. According to the Cambridge dictionary, "dog eat dog is used to describe a situation in which people will do anything to be successful, even if what they do harms other people."[15] While I agree this can happen, this does not need to be how Christians conduct their business.

The Bible does not say anything directly about business competition, although there are some references to athletic competition. For example, in a letter to the church at Corinth, the apostle Paul said, *Don't you realize that in a race everyone runs, but only one person gets the*

---

15. "Dog-Eat-Dog." Cambridge English Dictionary. Accessed March 2, 2021. https://dictionary.cambridge.org/us/dictionary/english/dog-eat-dog.

prize? So run to win! (1 Corinthians 9:24). While Paul was applying the race metaphor to his passion for sharing the good news of Jesus, it is clear that God wants us to be excellent in all our conduct, including in our business dealings. The pursuit of excellence is not to earn His favor (which is extended to us without charge) but to respond to His love (see Ephesians 2:8–10). The pressure of competition is intrinsically good because it reminds us to always put our best foot forward (see Romans 12:11). I will give the last word on this to Nancy Pearcey, well-known author and Christian thought leader: "Competition is always a good thing. It forces us to do our best. A monopoly renders people complacent and satisfied with mediocrity."

IS MONEY MORALLY GOOD?

An article by Tristin Hopper concerning food banks, published on December 6, 2018, in Canada's *National Post*, reminded me about the important role of money in any society.[16] As the lubricant of commerce, money is fundamentally good. Why? Because the existence of money is a precondition to efficient commerce, and commerce is critical to human flourishing. Therefore, money in itself is neither evil nor morally neutral but is instead a moral good. In the article, the author, while supportive of food drives as a means of helping food banks fulfill their mission, builds a formidable case for donating money rather than food. Donating cash rather than food is our normal practice with the local food bank. Here are some advantages that the article includes:

16. Tristin Hopper, "Help the Poor: Stop Donating Canned Goods to Food Banks," National Post, December 13, 2018. https://nationalpost.com/opinion/buying-canned-goods-to-donate-to-food-banks-is-inefficient-and-misguided-donate-money-instead.

- The food bank is much better at buying food than you are.
- Money doesn't have to be sorted and stored.
- You don't know what the food bank needs.

Prior to the invention of money as a medium of exchange, commerce took place through barter: my pigs for your potatoes. Because of obvious limitations like inadequate means of storage, transportation, and communication, the barter system was a huge barrier to human flourishing.

Thus, money is *the* essential lubricant for commerce anytime, anywhere. Without it, the tens of thousands of goods and services available today simply would not exist. So, while some look down on money (and by extension, business) as cut from ethically inferior cloth, the central role it plays is a great gift. Given the essential nature of money, an important function of modern governments through central banks is protecting their currencies from the ravages of inflation, including the hyperinflation running rampant in Venezuela at the time of this writing.

While money is morally good, the Bible has much to say about our attitude toward money. As Paul told his student, Timothy, it is the love of money (not money itself) that is *the root of all kinds of evil* (1 Timothy 6:10). Some have said that the lack of money is the root of all evil. I agree in the sense that the lack of money can stimulate a love of money that manifests in evil conduct such as theft and corruption.

As followers of Jesus, we must constantly remind ourselves that we are stewards, not owners. Since God the Creator owns everything (including money, represented in the Bible by silver and gold—see

Haggai 2:8), our duty and privilege are to use the money entrusted to us for His purposes. These purposes include not only meeting our own needs but also meeting the needs of others directly or indirectly by supporting good causes. Lastly, while money is good, its function is limited. As per the Beatles' 1964 hit song, money can't buy me love.

IS INEQUALITY OF POSSESSIONS MORALLY GOOD?

Based on media reports and editorial opinion, it would be natural to conclude that inequality of possessions is an obvious evil that must be righted. A brief Google search confirms that attacks on inequality are the norm. Of course, there is much inequality in the world. Mary and I have spent enough time among the very poor, not only in several developing countries but also on the streets of Toronto, to appreciate the magnitude of extreme economic inequality.

Most of the time, the root cause of grinding poverty in the developing world relates neither to business in general nor to evil multinational corporations but is often the product of inequality of opportunity resulting from a combination of totalitarian ideologies and corrupt leaders. In developed countries like Canada, poverty is caused or exacerbated by a multitude of factors, including poor individual choices, broken homes, ineffective government programs, and well-intended legislation that misses the mark.

Sometimes leaders attempt to level the economic playing field by using the power of the state. The most unfortunate recent example is Venezuela. Hugo Chavez, the country's late leader, said in an interview with ABC News, "I've been in revolt for years against ignominy, against injustice, against inequality, against immorality, against the exploitation of human beings."[17] While the idealism underlying these sentiments is laudable, Chavez's approach to correcting inequalities in Venezuela has effectively bankrupted what was once one of the world's wealthiest countries as measured by natural resources.

To be clear, the Bible strongly encourages followers of Jesus to take care of the poorest among us. The Bible also supports the notion that the inequalities that flow from the way God designed us are a moral good because humanity benefits as people strive to excel. Essentially, unequal outcomes are a function of unequal inputs.

Three relevant inputs come to mind. First, each of us is endowed by our Creator with different talents (see Romans 12:6–8). God's differential distribution of gifts is not unfair since He holds us to account only for our stewardship of the gifts with which He has entrusted us (see Matthew 25:14–30). Moreover, the possession of unique gifts should encourage us to use them to love others who do not have those specific gifts.

Second, God endows us with the freedom to choose whether or not to develop our talents. Sadly, many do not do so, and as a result, the world is poorer (to say nothing of those to whom the gifts have been given). Third, if we do not apply our gifts with energy and focus, nothing happens. The reward for nothing is nothing, which brings to mind some "professional students" I knew during my university days. I hope they ended up applying their many degrees to some useful purpose!

Some Christians point to pooling of resources in the early church as a model that the modern church should follow (see Acts 4:32–37).

17. "Transcript: Hugo Chavez Interview," ABC News Network. Accessed March 2, 2021. https://abcnews.go.com/Nightline/International/story?id=1134098&page=1.

They contend that this example affirms the moral goodness of redistribution of possessions to produce equal outcomes. This interpretation stretches the historical record. Unlike socialism, the communal sharing in the early church was voluntary, not coerced. Many followers of Jesus continued to own possessions, including their houses in which they met to worship God.

In short, while there are, of course, other aspects of business that are often seen as morally negative, or at best as morally neutral, such as the simple act of buying and selling, this analysis will hopefully help you engage in business unencumbered by a nagging feeling that it is somehow intrinsically morally tainted.

WAKE-UP CALL

Have you ever had misgivings about the intrinsic moral goodness of the for-profit business sector? If so, can you now see that the issue is not the system per se, but the issue is with those who lead within the system and the setting of their moral compass? Can you also see that private sector businesses, like all institutions within society, have their flaws, but there is no real-world utopian model to which one can appeal as a viable alternative to free-market capitalism, of which the linchpin is private sector business? In short, have you disentangled yourself from "the elephant in the room"?

To truly activate and sustain your calling to business leadership, a strong "why" is imperative, particularly given the real possibility that you will encounter opposition and even hostility. Let's now consider why everyone who has surrendered her or his life to Jesus *must* put Him first at work.

PART 2:
CALLED TO LOVE

WHY SHOULD I FOLLOW JESUS IN THE MARKETPLACE?

Chapter 3

THE GREAT WHY

"Love the Lord your God with all your heart and with all your soul and with all your mind." This is the first and greatest commandment. And the second is like it: "Love your neighbor as yourself." All the Law and the Prophets hang on these two commandments."

—JESUS (MATTHEW 22:37-40 NIV)

Why is openly living out our faith in the marketplace so daunting? After all, the Creator of everything has called us to represent Him there. What more motivation do we need? Many Christian marketplace leaders, however, tend to see themselves as secret agents in the workplace. Unlike Dan Aykroyd's character in the 1980 movie *The Blues Brothers*, we don't think, let alone declare, "We're on a mission from God!"[18]

18. *The Blues Brothers*, directed by John Landis (1980; Universal City, CA: Universal Studios, 2005), DVD.

WARNING: LANDMINES AHEAD!

The answer to these questions can be boiled down to fear of consequences. With good reason, we sense we are at war when we go into
the office. It is only natural to avoid conflicts related to our faith. After
all, we don't like getting hurt!

In his letter to the Ephesian church, Paul used a warfare analogy
to underscore this reality: *For we are not fighting against flesh-and-
blood enemies, but against evil rulers and authorities of the unseen world,
against mighty powers in this dark world, and against evil spirits in the
heavenly places* (Ephesians 6:12). Like the world at large, the marketplace is a spiritual battlefield in which one can be easily wounded.
Consequences range from simple rejection to more serious damage
like limiting our upward mobility and financial loss. Despite this,
we are called to continue marching forward, speaking boldly about
our faith.

Over the years, I have heard many excuses from leaders as to why
they cannot speak openly about their faith in the workplace. Many
of these reasons are couched in language that has a spiritual ring.
For example, "If my professional colleagues ask me how they can be
saved, I'll share the good news of Jesus Christ with them." This is most
unlikely to happen (particularly if these believers have been conducting themselves as secret agents), but it certainly sounds good! The best
excuse I have heard is, "I don't feel led by the Holy Spirit to openly
bring my faith into the office." It is a total discussion-ender—because
who is going to argue with the Holy Spirit, right?

Some people have even taken courses on evangelism but have not
yet shared the gospel with their peers in the marketplace. In this case,

their inaction is obviously not a lack of knowledge, but as earlier stated, it is fear of repercussions. A major reason they succumb to this fear is because they fail to understand that their options are binary; that is, they must either openly follow Jesus in the marketplace or openly follow Him in some other calling. After all, we are commanded to be "salt and light" wherever we are (Matthew 5:13–16). Similar to soldiers marching to war, we have been called to enter the battlefield of the marketplace by Jesus, our Commander in Chief!

If you find yourself struggling to bring your faith into the marketplace, this section will provide you with some compelling reasons to do just that. To begin, we must understand the lay of the land. If we are marching into battle in the workplace, we need to understand the battlefield. While I have lived in the United States and have done business extensively around the world, this discussion will focus primarily on what I have observed during my many years of involvement on the Canadian business scene. Having said that, though, the following generalizations concerning Canada and Canadian marketplace culture will resonate with readers in other countries, particularly in the West.

Like most economically advanced countries, Canada has become increasingly secular. Its institutions, including government, law courts, education, and business, have become more and more hostile to the Christian worldview. When I was growing up, Christianity was the principal religious practice in Canada. While most Canadians would not have said they were followers of Jesus, the majority were somewhat respectful of the Bible and its claim to authority. Today, the opposite is true.

In the public mind, biblical Christianity is deemed to be backward looking, closed-minded, and a barrier to social progress. Freedom of religion is coming under increasing attack by governments and the courts.[19] Ironically, this hostility is usually directed toward a caricature of historical Christianity. In fact, profound misunderstanding of Christian beliefs is pervasive among the populace at large, including leaders of influence (see chapter 4).

Since its founding, Canada has benefited from large inflows of immigrants from around the world. Most newcomers continue to live in accordance with the worldview of their homeland, which is usually not Christianity. As a result, religious pluralism, or the acceptance of all religious paths as equally valid, is upheld as a code of conduct to promote peaceful coexistence. Religious pluralism aside, the following are reasons for broadly based antipathy to the Christian worldview. Understanding them prepares us for the inevitable warfare when we openly honor the God of the Bible in the marketplace.

MEDIA CARICATURES

Throughout the West today, it is open season on all things Christian. The Christian worldview is often the object of ridicule and mockery by Hollywood, comedians, those in academia, and the general media. I have personally experienced this. Many years ago, at the urging of a member of my local church who was a writer for a national newspaper, we invited another writer from that publication to attend and report on a national conference of Christian business leaders that was

19. For example, Trinity Western University, a private Canadian university operating according to Christian principles, lost its legal battle to launch a law school in 2018 based upon a Supreme Court of Canada ruling that it was "proportionate and reasonable" to limit religious rights to ensure open access for LGBT students. Specifically, the court ruled that the university could not impose a code of conduct that prohibited sexual relations outside the sanctity of marriage between one man and one woman.

being hosted by me and another CEO. The article appeared across Canada the following week on the front page of the business section. It included several factual errors and seemingly went out of the way to present the attendees and content of the sessions in a biased and negative light.

The scornful attitude frequently expressed in the media is ironic given that most countries in the West were founded on Christian ethical values. Many of the world's most well-known universities, including Oxford and Cambridge in the UK, Harvard and Princeton in the US, and the Universities of Toronto and Ottawa in Canada, even explicitly acknowledged their Christian center at the time they were established.

CHRISTIAN BEHAVIOR

When criticizing the Christian worldview, antagonists frequently cite what they perceive to be unacceptable behavior of self-proclaimed Christians. However, for believers, criticism, even persecution, should come as no surprise. Jesus Himself clearly warned that just as He was persecuted, so, too, would His followers be persecuted (see Matthew 5:10–12; John 15:20).

Of course, in some cases, observations about misconduct might be accurate. These accusations actually serve to underscore a key tenet of the Christian faith—that everyone messes up on a regular basis and, as a result, needs forgiveness. So however unfortunate it might be, it is not surprising when some who claim to be Jesus' followers engage in actions that are not in accordance with Jesus' teaching.

It is important to remember that this truth about human nature does not negate the truth-claims of the Christian worldview. People often confuse the misbehavior of Christians with the message of Jesus. This is a profound error. The core beliefs of the Christian worldview are based upon the person of Jesus, including His claims, conduct, teachings, and, supremely, His sacrificial death to rescue all who put their trust in Him and His subsequent resurrection from the dead. On this score, it is claimed that Mahatma Gandhi once said, "I did once seriously think of embracing the Christian faith. The gentle figure of Christ, so full of forgiveness that He taught His followers not to retaliate when abused or struck, but to turn the other cheek—I thought it was a beautiful example of the perfect man."[20]

As a Christian, I feel ashamed of the misdeeds of Christians whose words and actions have brought Jesus' name into disrepute. While some of these failures of self-proclaiming Christians have been exaggerated or have not been judged objectively within a proper historical context, the genuine harm caused cannot be excused. This mistrust, misunderstanding, and hostility toward religion (specifically Christianity) has virtually turned secular humanism into the state-sponsored religion of the West, sitting comfortably alongside religious pluralism. We will discuss secularist objections to Christianity later in the book, but understanding the general perception of those outside of the Christian community can better equip us as we both live out and share our faith with those we encounter in the marketplace.

20. Roland Spliesgart, "India: Gandhi on Christianity," in *A History of Christianity in Asia, Africa, and Latin America, 1450-1990: A Documentary Sourcebook*, edited by Klaus Koschorke, Frieder Ludwig, and Mariano Delgado. (Grand Rapids: Eerdmans, 2007), 109.

Of course, it can be a challenging endeavor, for this hostility toward Christianity often creates so-called landmines for leaders in the marketplace who desire to be open about their faith. While these landmines have many different labels, such as political correctness or identity politics, they all have one thing in common: they promote what is deemed to be acceptable speech.

Generally speaking, the Christian worldview is seen as off limits. Rather than encouraging the respectful debate of different perspectives, the proponents of "correct" speech categorize the person holding other views as morally deficient. The labels ascribed to Christians are usually not based on evidence of improper conduct but rather reflect a negative judgment of the person's character based solely upon the beliefs they espouse, or are based upon immutable factors such as race, gender, or sexual orientation.

THE LARGEST BATTLEFIELD

Though the workplace may feel like a vast and daunting battlefield, the largest battlefield is not actually the workplace but our minds. Thoughts precede actions, and wrong thinking begets wrong actions. In this regard, we need to be constantly aware that Satan's most effective ploy is to contaminate our thinking with his lies. His goal is to persuade us to not pursue a marketplace calling but rather to leave God at home. Being the father of lies (see John 8:44), Satan seeks to instill a fear of negative repercussions that renders us harmless to his cause.

As with all plausible lies, there is an element of truth. There is the possibility that we will be hurt. However, we believers have not been given *a spirit of fear, but of power and of love and of a sound mind* (see

2 Timothy 1:7 NKJV). The best antidote to Satan's lies is to implement a twofold strategy. First, we must continually renew our minds by filling them with truth. According to Jesus, we are sanctified by the truth when we read and absorb God's Word (see John 17:17). Second, we must be passionately motivated by the most compelling reason for following Jesus in the marketplace.

THE GREAT WHY

This chapter opened with Jesus' response to a lawyer's question concerning the most important commandment in the law of Moses. Commonly referred to as the Great Commandment, it declares that we are to love God with everything we've got, and we are to love others as ourselves. For purposes of this chapter, the Great Commandment will be relabeled the Great Why. We could say the Great Why is Jesus' fundamental rule of life. Therefore, all who claim to be His follower in whatever professional and personal capacity they find themselves are called to obey this one commandment.

HOW DO WE LOVE GOD?

In the fourteenth chapter of the book of John, Jesus provides a very concise directive concerning how we are to love God. Given the religious milieu of the time, one might have expected Him to emphasize the importance of following all the rules laid out in the Hebrew Scriptures. While the New Testament tells us that Jesus obeyed every one of these rules perfectly, He didn't expect us to perfectly follow His example in respect of the law. In fact, He simply said we love God by obeying Him (Jesus). This point is so profound that John repeats it five times in that one chapter.

It follows that our practices in the marketplace are not good if they are not done in obedience to the leading of the Holy Spirit. This includes the generous giving of our time, influence, finances, and expertise. Of course, God wants us to give generously of the resources with which He has entrusted us. However, just because we deem certain things meritorious does not make them good by God's standards. Rather, He wants us to use our resources to support those causes He designates. They extend, most importantly, to our interactions with others since He commands us to love our neighbours as ourselves.

HOW DO WE LOVE OUR NEIGHBORS?

If we reframe the Great Why to say that we love God by loving others, yet we don't love those with whom we interact in the marketplace, then we do not love God since we are not obeying Jesus' command. Do I hear an "ouch" from anyone else? According to Andy Stanley in his book *Irresistible*,[21] in every circumstance we need to ask the question "What does love require of me?" Then we should act accordingly.

In Paul's first letter to the church at Corinth, he wrote:

> *If I could speak all the languages of earth and of angels,*
> *but didn't love others, I would only be a noisy gong or*
> *a clanging cymbal. If I had the gift of prophecy, and*
> *if I understood all of God's secret plans and possessed*

21. Andy Stanley, *Irresistible: Reclaiming the New that Jesus Unleashed for the World* (Grand Rapids: Zondervan, 2018).

all knowledge, and if I had such faith that I could move mountains, but didn't love others, I would be nothing. If I gave everything I have to the poor and even sacrificed my body, I could boast about it; but if I didn't love others, I would have gained nothing.
(1 Corinthians 13:1–3)

One way of reading Paul's exhortation is to substitute the words "allow God to live through me to" for the word "love." After all, being love Himself, God is the ultimate source of perfect love (see 1 John 4:8). We could rephrase 1 Corinthians 13:2 as, "If I didn't [allow God to live through me to] others, I would be nothing!" By extension, we cannot love others solely through our philanthropy and other good deeds. They might have merit in the world's eyes, but if they are not done according to the leading of the Holy Spirit, they are not truly God's love in action, and we gain nothing from them.

Since we are Jesus' ambassadors to the marketplace, love requires that we consistently reveal God to all those with whom we interact. We reveal Him by exhibiting the fruit of His indwelling Holy Spirit, obeying the Great Commandment—the Great Why—and sharing the good news of salvation through Jesus Christ.

EXHIBITING THE FRUIT OF THE SPIRIT

According to Paul in his letter to the Galatian church, the fruit of the Holy Spirit is *love, joy, peace, patience, kindness, goodness, faithfulness, gentleness, and self-control* (Galatians 5:22–23). Based upon this, two immediate observations come to mind.

First, this fruit is produced by the Holy Spirit living inside every believer. As we discussed earlier, this is not simply a matter of exercising the power of positive thinking. It is the direct result of allowing Jesus to live through us. For example, during the Great Recession in 2008, when it seemed that the global economy was on the brink of collapse, the peace of God inside me was on display to my colleagues in my investment management company in the midst of the extraordinary volatility in the capital markets.

In a similar manner, God's peace enveloped me three years later when my doctor told me I had lung cancer. In the days following this diagnosis, the peace I was experiencing was quite evident to everyone, including my doctor and my business associates. The reason my behavior stood out as different is because, for many people, the words "you have cancer" evoke a sense of fear, not peace.[22] While I fully understood that Jesus was my security in the midst of these storms, the peace I was experiencing didn't flow from my reasoning faculties. Rather, it was the peace flowing from the Holy Spirit in me.

This type of peace is not available to those who do not believe in Jesus. It can only be experienced if we have become His followers and carry the promise that He will make His home in us (see Galatians 2:20). In the two significant challenges I mentioned, as well as many others over the years, I used the alarming nature of the situation as an opportunity to point people to Jesus as the source of my peace. While some people did not receive Jesus upon my witness, I knew I was planting seeds of faith.

Second, love is the first fruit on the list. This fact ties neatly to

22. Thankfully, God healed me through the services of a very talented thoracic surgeon, and I have been completely cancer-free for many years!

both Paul's letter to the Corinthian church, wherein love is the greatest virtue, and to the Great Why articulated by Jesus Himself. Very conveniently, Paul provides us with a detailed picture of love in the same letter to the Corinthians:

> *Love is patient and kind. Love is not jealous or boastful or proud or rude. It does not demand its own way. It is not irritable, and it keeps no record of being wronged. It does not rejoice about injustice but rejoices whenever the truth wins out. Love never gives up, never loses faith, is always hopeful, and endures through every circumstance.* (1 Corinthians 13:4–7)

Applying Andy Stanley's rule to this list, we could say that love requires us to follow, in each and every circumstance, the way of patience, kindness, contentment, humility, selflessness, forgiving others, doing the right thing, speaking the truth in love, perseverance, constancy in our faith, and hopefulness. There is some overlap between this list and the fruit of the Spirit, which again underscores the Great Why, that love should underpin every facet of our lives as we seek to follow Jesus.

LIVING BY THE GOLDEN RULE

The Golden Rule (hereafter "the Rule") is based upon Jesus' directive: *So in everything, do to others what you would have them do to you, for this sums up the Law and the Prophets* (Matthew 7:12, NIV). Many believe that the Rule is common to all major worldviews, but this is simply not true. While many other worldviews espouse philosophies that superficially resemble the Rule, they are, in fact, profoundly different.

In essence, Jesus is instructing us to engage in selfless generosity. Put differently, He is encouraging us to put the other person's interests ahead of our own, even if it might disadvantage us in some way. The most common variations of the Rule outside the Christian worldview focus on reciprocity, which means that we put others first if it is to our personal advantage. Importantly, the Rule often clashes with current marketplace culture. For example, how does one square maximizing return on investment and profitability with putting the interests of others first? While the Rule applies to every aspect of our conduct in the marketplace, I want us to focus on the Rule in respect to our employees and customers.

According to the Rule, Jesus challenges us to genuinely look out for the best interests of our employees. Let's consider this in the context of regular employee performance reviews. Every business in which I have been involved followed this practice annually. From experience, this review could sometimes become an uncomfortable conversation about unacceptable performance. There is often a bias in business against transparency during performance reviews. This tendency is often motivated by conflict avoidance. In addition, fear of losing employees whose work, while not fully satisfactory, is acceptable overall, is sometimes a motivator. A common outcome of this thinking is "halo reviews," where one would be hard-pressed to find a critical or corrective comment, even if clearly warranted!

Untruthful halo reviews are inconsistent with the Rule. If we are actually interested in helping our employees grow, candid feedback might be precisely what is in their best interests. After I became a Christian, I decided to regularly pray for my employees and my interactions with them. My goal was to provide feedback that would help them succeed, recognizing that candor carries risk. To be effective, of course, such feedback must be accompanied by trust between employee and supervisor.

Regarding customers, my comments will focus on the investment industry, but the principles discussed are broadly applicable to other industries. As it happens, my industry, like many others, is highly regulated. In a way, securities regulation is the government's attempt to impose the Rule. In fact, if all participants in the industry were motivated by the Rule, no regulation would be necessary.

Let's consider the Rule in the context of the relationship between investment advisers and their clients. In Canadian law, advisers have an obligation, or fiduciary duty, to act in their clients' best interests. This duty is intended to protect investors from decisions by their advisers that benefit them rather than their clients. An obvious area of concern is activity in client accounts that is motivated primarily by commissions to the adviser rather than whether the investment is suitable for the client's account. In fact, registered investment advisers in Canadian firms are required to have a clear understanding of their clients' needs, including their investment goals and their appetite for risk. Notwithstanding, all investment firms must have compliance departments since not every adviser abides by these rules.

The reality is that externally imposed rules can change behaviors but not hearts. The Rule is really a matter of the heart. Either we genuinely care for our clients or we don't. If, in our hearts, we are not concerned for their best interests, there is a tension between externally imposed rules and our inner motivation. The motives of the heart often seek to comply with the letter of the law while circumventing its intent. Since Jesus' commandment dealt with the attitude of our heart, He focused on the spirit of the rules rather than the letter. This focus deals with the sometimes very uncomfortable subject of motive, which can lead to unethical conduct.

There are many today who confuse the message of Jesus with a list of compliance rules. However, He really came to make a relationship with God possible as a direct result of our decision to put Him in charge of our lives. This new relationship with Him then impacts how we treat others. My behavior does not always match my new worldview, and there are times when a self-centered motive gets the better of me; however, Jesus, in His perfection, always knows what is best for me and nudges me in that direction.

As I listen to Him, my attitudes change and my compliance with the Golden Rule improves. In the following Bible passage, the apostle Paul describes this internal transformation as the renewing of our minds as our knowledge of Jesus grows: *Do not conform to the pattern of this world, but be transformed by the renewing of your mind. Then you will be able to test and approve what God's will is—his good, pleasing and perfect will* (Romans 12:2, NIV).

Of course, as stated earlier, loving God by loving others can be expensive. First, it puts us at risk of rejection and other negative consequences, such as losing employees or income. Second, it often requires tangible sacrifices flowing directly from our use of the various different resources entrusted to our stewardship. Rather than using our time, talent, and treasure exclusively to satisfy our own needs and wants, we are to use them to love others (see chapter 12). For business and other marketplace leaders, "others" means everyone we serve, including customers, employees, shareholders, creditors, and suppliers. Without God, this feat is impossible, but the Bible reassures us that with Him leading us, all things are possible.

WAKE-UP CALL

Several years ago, I attended a dinner with Mary in Oxford, England, in conjunction with a Christian apologetics program for marketplace leaders. We sat with a former successful businessman who now shares his faith in Christ as an international speaker.

At one point during the evening, he made the following startling assertion (paraphrased): "If believers are not constantly sharing their faith with everyone, including their marketplace peers, they don't understand the gospel." In essence, he was saying that the good news of Jesus Christ is so overwhelmingly good that it should be impossible not to share it. In a similar vein, I heard of a well-known evangelist who, after having spoken to large audiences over many decades, concluded that it is not just unbelievers who need the gospel. Believers also need a constant refresher in the gospel and its implications.

This brings to mind what Peter and John told their persecutors who forbade them from mentioning Jesus in the marketplace after they healed a lame man in Jesus' name: *As for us, we cannot help speaking about what we have seen and heard* (Acts 4:20 NIV). If we truly love those around us, and if we truly understand the profound message of the gospel, we will not be able to keep quiet about it when we are around our peers and colleagues. In the context of your marketplace, are you loving your peers?

Chapter 4
THE GREATEST WHY

How much do you have to hate somebody to
believe that everlasting life is possible and not
tell them that?

—PENN JILLETTE, ATHEIST

It is ironic that Penn Jillette, an outspoken atheist, has highlighted the truth of our purpose as Christians in a video blog published in 2010. At first blush, his use of the word "hate" to make his point might seem excessive. However, it is difficult for any believer not to be convicted by Jillette's irrefutable logic. Alternatively, it might be that we don't yet fully understand (or dare I say, believe) the breathtaking greatness of our salvation (see 1 Peter 1:10–12) and its implications for those with whom we interact in our professional lives.

While everything believers do in the marketplace should glorify God, there is nothing that brings Him more glory than playing our assigned role in bringing Jesus the reward for His sufferings. Of course, God will often prompt us by the Holy Spirit to perform acts of compassion and kindness. The direct impact of these commendable actions, however, pales in comparison with the impact of helping others to see that everlasting life with a loving, perfect heavenly Father is possible. After all, the former has temporal consequences, while the latter has eternal consequences. To say it differently, life on Earth is full of pain, suffering, and evil, and we are called in many different ways to do our part in righting wrongs. However, in the context of eternity, our physical existence on Earth is short and fleeting.

Of course, it is Jesus, not us, who saves through the ministry of the Holy Spirit. In His infinite wisdom, God has chosen to employ agents (us) to share His message of salvation by grace through faith in Jesus with marketplace leaders. We might not lead someone with whom we share the good news to receive Jesus as Lord and Savior, but that reality does not exempt us from our responsibility to speak truth into the lives of leaders, particularly those with whom we have relational equity. The popular phrase "speaking truth to power" comes to mind since marketplace leaders are powerful. While we are all called to sow, Jesus makes it clear that we will not always reap the harvest (see John 4:35–38).

For some reason, many Christians ascribe greater merit to taking the gospel to the poor and marginalized than to CEOs and other marketplace leaders. However, Jesus is an equal opportunity lover. He doesn't love the beggar living in a slum in Bangladesh any more than the CEO of a major multinational corporation. While most CEOs are much better off materially than believers I have met in the favelas of Brazil or the slums of New Delhi, they are spiritually impoverished compared with their Christian counterparts in developing countries.

Given our proximity to those who are wealthy by this world's standards, however, God has given us the special privilege of reaching our "poverty stricken" peers as follows:

> *All authority in heaven and on earth has been given to me. Therefore go and make disciples of all nations, baptizing them in the name of the Father and of the Son and of the Holy Spirit, and teaching them to obey everything I have commanded you. And surely I am with you always, to the very end of the age.* (Matthew 28:18–20 NIV)

These words are commonly called "the Great Commission." Of special note, Jesus' instructions cannot be construed as "the Great Suggestion" or "the Great Recommendation"!

As explained in chapter 3, we love God by obeying Jesus. Moreover, Jesus did not direct this command at a special subset of followers. Rather the "go" in this command is directed at every single believer in Jesus, including all marketplace leaders—from CEOs on down. No one is exempt. However, Jesus is not sending us on a solo assignment. Rather, He is with us always through the indwelling Holy Spirit. According to author Ed Silvoso, the Great Commission should probably be relabeled "the Great Partnership."[23]

Excuses like "I'm not called to evangelism," "Sharing the good news about Jesus is not my gifting," or "If you understood the environment at my company, you would appreciate the impossibility of my obeying this command at work" can sound reasonable and even somewhat spiritual. However, they fly in the face of Jesus' rule that

23. Ed Silvoso, *Ekklesia: Rediscovering God's Instrument for Global Transformation* (Ada: Baker Publishing Group), 2017.

we love God by loving others. If we truly believe that those who don't respond to Jesus' offer of reconciliation will be eternally separated from God, it follows that we love them first and foremost by sharing the gospel of God's grace. When it comes to the rationale for following Jesus in the marketplace, the primary reason is the Great Commission.

Of course, our employer did not appoint us to a leadership role for the express purpose of sharing our faith in God with others. Within the framework of our duty to our employer, however, we are called by Jesus to share the gospel. Later in this book, we will discuss practical suggestions for maximizing sharing opportunities while honoring our employers.

Why me? There are two main reasons why Jesus gave us this important assignment. First, marketplace leaders around the world are an unreached people group. Second, the Christian leader is best positioned to reach his peers with the message of Jesus.

MARKETPLACE LEADERS ARE AN UNREACHED PEOPLE GROUP

While most countries in the West have a Judeo-Christian heritage, this fact does not mean that everyone has already heard the good news. In fact, the opposite is true. Having spent time in various developing nations among people who have never heard the gospel, I can assure you that marketplace leaders are often equally ignorant. Actually, in some respect, they are more ignorant since their minds are frequently cluttered with a caricature of the Christian worldview that must first be dispelled before they can receive the genuine article. By contrast, their unreached counterparts in the developing world are often hearing the message of Jesus for the very first time—and they know good news when they hear it!

In my experience, the overwhelming majority of marketplace leaders have never heard a clear exposition of the gospel for a couple of reasons. First, they have not felt the need to explore the big questions of life, such as where we came from, why we are here, how we should live, and where we are going. Second, no one credible has shared the gospel with them.

The avoidance of deep conversations by non-believers comes with many excuses—busyness being one of the most common. Given the frenetic pace of life today, many leaders tend to be distracted by what they perceive to be more relevant and pressing concerns and desires that seemingly demand their attention. Moreover, the energy they expend simply getting through each day often leaves them feeling drained of the strength and emotional resources to tackle such questions, particularly the need for critical thinking and self-assessment.

Some people justify avoidance based upon their perception that these questions are a philosophical exercise without application in the "real world" in which they live. The absence of any felt need often breeds inertia. In many cases, it is only when people are engulfed by a life crisis that these deep questions bubble to the surface.[24]

Another reason for avoidance is comfort with the status quo. Life just works for many marketplace leaders, even though they know that not everything is perfect. In this context, acknowledging they don't have it all together or under complete control is unsettling, even frightening. Ironically (confident outward demeanour

---

24. These crises are usually related to problems—such as drug addiction, a death in the family, run-ins with the law, serious health problems, termination of employment, bankruptcy, and divorce. However, they can also be related to success. As discussed in the introduction, I suddenly found myself wondering about the meaning of my own life after a major accomplishment. The realization that professional success and its rewards were not as satisfying as I had anticipated motivated me to consider other sources of fulfillment.

notwithstanding), anyone in senior leadership is more acutely aware than most that they don't know it all. In fact, they are often quite uncertain as to the best course of action.

Finally, some leaders are not particularly open to the views of others who don't share their background. They question whether input from pastors, philosophers, or theologians is relevant since they believe such individuals do not understand their world.

Additionally, most marketplace leaders are an unreached people group due to the fact that no one has clearly explained the gospel to them and differentiated it from common misperceptions. Based upon my experience, I believe that most people who are not followers of Jesus don't understand the core beliefs of the Christian faith—not even close. In my travels around the world, I have found this statement to be universally true—irrespective of race, culture, or religious background (or lack thereof).

In support of this assertion concerning the widespread incomprehension of the Christian worldview, the following is a conversation I have had on occasion with other marketplace leaders (ML) who were not at that time followers of Jesus. Importantly, these individuals were open to this conversation since they knew me and considered me credible based upon our professional relationship.

Me: Would you mind if I ran a hypothesis by you?

ML: Sure.

Me: My hypothesis is that the overwhelming majority of business executives in these downtown office towers don't really know what Christianity is all about. They likely have some perceptions about Christianity shaped by the media and the behavior of people who claim to be Christians, but they have never applied themselves to understanding the central claims of the Christian worldview. Would you agree?

ML: [after a pause] Yes.

Me: Would you mind if I briefly shared those core beliefs?

ML: Sure.

In the conversation above, why does my business colleague pause before agreeing with the hypothesis? The reason is because he or she realizes in that moment that the answer to the question is binary—either yes or no. They know they cannot really articulate the core tenets of the Christian worldview, and since it is human nature to avoid putting one's ignorance on display, they usually feel their only option is to answer yes. Their willingness to admit ignorance and to listen to my explanation has led to some interesting conversations. In some cases, it has resulted in their believing in Jesus.

Some people hide their discomfort about engaging in such conversations by saying their strategy for sharing the gospel is to let their light shine through exemplary conduct. By doing this, they hope their peers will be stimulated to ask why they behave the way they do, ultimately asking what they must do to be saved. Of course, as ambassadors of Christ, we must always conduct ourselves in a way that honors God. With that said, there are many people who live moral lives, but that doesn't usually cause others to ask them why they do so. This strategy brings to mind the saying (sometimes improperly attributed to St. Francis of Assisi) "Preach the gospel at all times, and if necessary, use words." With due respect to the author of this exhortation, words are always necessary when preaching the gospel.

Here is a thought experiment. Visualize three spiritually minded marketplace leaders sitting in a boardroom. By spiritually minded, I mean that all three acknowledge the existence of God and desire to please Him. However, they have never heard a clear exposition of the gospel. Their purpose is to determine the best way to achieve reconciliation with God. During their brainstorming session, what are the odds one of them will say something along the following lines: "I have a great idea! Let's ask God to become a man, lead a morally perfect life, take all our sins upon Himself by dying for us, and rise from the dead to validate the meaning of His death and assure us that we, too, will one day be resurrected in like manner"? I think we can all agree that the probability of this scenario is zero! There is no way around it. No one will ever come up with God's plan of salvation through intellectual reasoning.

They can, however, use their minds to investigate the facts backing up the gospel. For example, the resurrection of Jesus is based upon historical records that have been exhaustively studied down through the centuries (see chapter 7). However, the truth of the gospel must ultimately be spiritually discerned, and the catalyst is the preaching (i.e., telling, not teaching) of the message of salvation combined with the convicting work of the Holy Spirit. In Paul's words:

> How then shall they call on Him in whom they have not believed? And how shall they believe in Him of whom they have not heard? And how shall they hear without a preacher? And how shall they preach unless they are sent? As it is written: "How beautiful are the feet of those who preach the gospel of peace, who bring glad tidings of good things!" But they have not all obeyed the gospel. For Isaiah says,

"Lord, who has believed our report?" So then faith comes by hearing, and hearing by the word of God. (Romans 10:14–17 NKJV)

Earlier in his letter to the Romans, Paul makes a point that is often overlooked. The preaching of the gospel carries spiritual power to convert others to believe in Jesus. Specifically, Paul says, *For I am not ashamed of the gospel of Christ, for it is the* power of God *to salvation for everyone who believes, for the Jew first and also for the Greek* (Romans 1:16 NKJV, emphasis added). In some mysterious way, the Holy Spirit acts on the hearers to convict them of the truth of their need for a rescuer because of their sin. While I can't explain how this works, I know from experience that it is true. Over the years, I have both seen and heard about some very smart, accomplished people who, after hearing the gospel, have cast aside their intellectual doubts and embraced Jesus as their Lord and Savior.

MARKETPLACE LEADERS ARE BEST POSITIONED TO REACH THEIR PEERS

When I was growing up, it was not uncommon for people to come to faith through the preaching of an evangelist like Billy Graham. While this still happens today, it is much less common, particularly in the West. The reality is that most marketplace leaders are unlikely to attend a crusade or darken the door of a church. This does not mean, however, that they are closed to hearing the gospel. Recall that many of them cannot see relevance in religion, even though in quiet moments they know something is missing from their lives. However, they usually feel they cannot disclose their weaknesses for fear of possible negative consequences, including ceding power to others. So they put on a mask that communicates fulfilled individuals who are confident in their ability to lead their followers into a successful future.

The reality is that many are living in a self-imposed prison, feeling that there is no one with whom they can share their fears and problems. That, my friend, is why God has called you to business! After all, you have found your faith to be highly relevant to your own professional and personal life. Moreover, unlike a pastor or even a gifted evangelist like Billy Graham, you have credibility with your peers since you share their background and experience. Assuming you are representing Jesus well in the marketplace, you might be the only person who can reach them with the gospel!

POWER TO SHARE

The previous section makes the case that the central purpose of a business calling is to share the gospel with those with whom we have influence. This "Greatest Why" will not, however, accomplish anything in and of itself. First, we must act on it. Second, we must be empowered to share. I will make the argument that we must not only be motivated, but we must also be especially empowered by God to share the gospel effectively and frequently. In other words, His power, which is separate and distinct from our own personal abilities, must be harnessed to impact others with the gospel.

Power makes the world move. Imagine Jesus' day for a moment, when power to accomplish physical tasks came from the muscles of the people or the animals serving them. Fast forward to the twenty-first century. The vast improvement in living standards over the previous two millennia wouldn't have happened without harnessing many different power sources that were developed through advancing technology.

Just as power is necessary to accomplish physical work, it is also necessary to accomplish spiritual work. Knowing that His followers would face many obstacles as they engaged with non-believers in a hostile culture, Jesus told His followers they would need additional spiritual power to accomplish the mission He was giving them. While the words of the gospel carry their own power (see Romans 1:16), Jesus knew that His followers would need something extra to be effective witnesses. He did not want to leave us entirely dependent upon our own devices.

That "something extra" was not a degree in theology. Based upon the New Testament record, this something extra was baptism in the Holy Spirit ("the Baptism"). While many Christians today do not accept the Baptism and the accompanying gifts of the Holy Spirit as continuing subsequent to the death of the last apostle, it is certainly a matter of historical record in both the gospel accounts and the apostolic letters, as well as in the writings of the early church fathers.[25]

In fact, all four gospel accounts proclaim that Jesus will baptize His followers with the Holy Spirit. For example, in Matthew's

---

25. There are two theological camps regarding the Baptism. Those who believe that the gifts of the Spirit are not in operation today are labeled "cessationists," while those who believe the gifts are in operation today are labeled "continuationists." Both camps anchor their positions in scriptural arguments. Having studied the issue in some depth, I am of the view that the argument favoring continuationism is the stronger of the two based primarily on Scripture and secondarily on experience. For a scholarly argument supporting continuationism, please see Dr. Sam Storms's article titled "Why I Am a Continuationist." For the counterargument, see Dr. Thomas Schreiner's article "Why I Am a Cessationist."

account, John the Baptist says, *I baptize with water those who repent of their sins and turn to God. But someone is coming soon who is greater than I am—so much greater that I'm not worthy even to be His slave and carry His sandals. He will baptize you with the Holy Spirit and with fire* (Matthew 3:11). By contrast, only the Gospel of John describes Jesus as the Lamb of God who takes away the sin of the world, a concept well understood and accepted by all believers.

To be clear, every single believer in Jesus is indwelt by the Holy Spirit of God. The moment individuals turn away from their old life and believe in Jesus, they receive the Holy Spirit, their identity changes, and their eternal destiny as God's children is completely secure. For example, in John's account, the believers received the Holy Spirit as follows: *And with that he [Jesus] breathed on them and said, "Receive the Holy Spirit"* (John 20:22, NIV). These realities are not dependent upon receiving the Baptism. Moreover, the power of the Holy Spirit is within them—provided they avail themselves of it. Therefore, there is no such thing as a second-class Christian.

However, scholars generally agree that the Baptism first occurred at Pentecost. Since this event took place subsequent to Jesus' followers "receiving the Holy Spirit" according to the account in John's Gospel, the Baptism is a separate and distinct experience from the initial receiving of the Holy Spirit. In the book of Acts, Luke records an incident that occurred subsequent to Jesus' resurrection and prior to His ascension: *On one occasion, while he [Jesus] was eating with them, he gave them this command: "Do not leave Jerusalem, but wait for the gift my Father promised, which you have heard me speak about. For John baptized with water, but in a few days you will be baptized with the Holy Spirit"* (Acts 1:4–5, NIV).

In the first chapter of Acts, we learn why Jesus commanded His disciples to receive the Baptism:

> *Then they gathered around him and asked him, "Lord, are you at this time going to restore the kingdom to Israel?" He said to them: "It is not for you to know the times or dates the Father has set by his own authority.* But* you will receive power when the Holy Spirit comes on you; *and you will be my witnesses in Jerusalem, and in all Judea and Samaria, and to the ends of the earth."* (Acts 1:6–8, emphasis added)

In essence, Jesus was telling them that prior to His return they needed to be empowered to witness. To reiterate, any born-again person has the Holy Spirit and can share the gospel with anyone. Some Christians who don't believe in the Baptism are very effective in their witness. However, Jesus Himself said that believers need to receive the Baptism to witness most effectively, and who are we to argue with Jesus, who is *the same yesterday, today, and forever* (Hebrews 13:8)? One way to understand the distinction between initially receiving the Holy Spirit and the subsequent baptism in the Holy Spirit is that the first is characterized by *new life* and the second is characterized by *new power*.

Of particular relevance to this argument is the fact that the disciples rejoiced and praised God enthusiastically between the time of their encounter with the resurrected Jesus and the day of Pentecost. However, it was only subsequent to the Holy Spirit's falling on them at Pentecost that they began witnessing to others about Jesus. For example, Peter retired permanently from fishing (for the second time!),[26] and he never looked back following the Baptism with the evidence of speaking in other tongues. After the second chapter of Acts, the concept of receiving the Holy Spirit is not used in the context of conversion but only in the context of the Baptism.[27] The visible sign that other believers received the Baptism was speaking in tongues.

In the first week following my encounter with the person of Jesus, a group of believers, including my wife, Mary, laid hands on me and prayed for me to receive the baptism in the Holy Spirit. As I was already eager for everything God had in store for me, I was more than ready to receive, and I did so immediately with the evidence of speaking in other tongues. I was immediately infused with a boldness to witness to anyone anywhere about the love of Jesus, which has continued up to the present day. And I often pray in tongues prior to sharing my faith with others, albeit silently if I am in their presence. Over the years, I have shared my faith in Jesus with CEOs and other senior executives, as well as just about anyone else with whom I have come into contact from all walks of life. That said, I would emphasize that there have been many godly men and women down through the centuries who did not speak in tongues but nevertheless knew the power of God in their lives.

WAKE-UP CALL

As leaders, we are given the very special privilege of sharing the gospel with our peers in the marketplace. We are not exempt from this

26. Recall from John 21 that a dispirited Peter went back to fishing, his former occupation!
27. See accounts in Acts 8, 10, and 19. In every case, the apostles, who themselves had been baptized in the Holy Spirit at Pentecost, recognized others as having also received the baptism in the Holy Spirit when they spoke in other tongues.

assignment based upon the fact that the marketplace culture in the twenty-first century is a virtual minefield. In fact, sharing the gospel is the ultimate expression of our love for God and for others. According to Penn Jillette, if we don't share the gospel, we must ask ourselves if we genuinely love our neighbor.

Do you regularly share the gospel with your peers in the marketplace? If not, why not? After all, Jesus commands us to love others by sharing His good news with them. If you agree that the Great Commandment is an order and not a suggestion but you still don't share the gospel, is it possible you need a spiritual boost? Have you availed yourself of God's power by asking Jesus to baptize you in His Holy Spirit so that His words to others spill out of the overflow in you?

Chapter 5

MORE THAN YOUR BUSINESS CARD

In our production-oriented society, being busy, having an occupation, has become one of the main ways, if not the main way, of identifying ourselves. Without an occupation, not just our economic security but our very identity is endangered.

–HENRI NOUWEN

From decades of corporate leadership experience, I have concluded that the identity of many leaders is tightly bound up in their business cards. In my experience, this assertion even holds true for some leaders who profess to be followers of Jesus. I have known or know of senior executives whose identities seemingly imploded when they were fired or retired of their own choice. Many senior executives discover at a certain point that those with whom they dealt in business were interested in them primarily for what they could do for them. When they no longer occupy their position of authority, the phone seldom rings. For some, this reality can be deeply troubling. They can feel disoriented, even somewhat lost.

In most worldviews, identity is *achieved*. In Christianity, identity is *received*. The starting point for leaders who desire to honor Jesus in the marketplace is a deep internalization of the true identity they have received in Christ. An accurate perception of that identity and its implications is the foundation that underpins our behavior at home, in the marketplace, and in society. This perception plays a huge role in shaping our response to opportunities and crises. Most importantly, it informs how we treat and lead others. In a way, our internalized identity is akin to the operating system on a computer. It works behind the scenes to ensure that everything in our life functions properly, by which I mean in accordance with God's will. In the context of the Great Why and the Greatest Why, we must remain authentic to our true identity.

My own identity prior to encountering Jesus was based primarily upon how much I achieved in life and how others responded to my achievements. I thought the road to fulfillment was personal performance. By performing with excellence, my craving for self-worth and the recognition of others was satisfied, as was my desire for affirmation through financial reward and advancement in the corporate world. I remember receiving newly minted Citibank business cards informing me and the world that I was vice president. It should be noted that while there was only one president of Citibank New York, there were quite a few of us vice presidents around the world. That did not matter, though, for I owned my title and it made me feel important. For a young man in the 1970s, this was impressive stuff. In so many ways, my business card became my identity. Can you relate?

However, my self-perception changed radically when Jesus came into my life. In Paul's letter to the church in Corinth, he describes the transformation I underwent:

> *Either way, Christ's love controls us. Since we believe that Christ died for all, we also believe that we have all died to our old life. He died for everyone so that those who receive His new life will no longer live for themselves. Instead, they will live for Christ, who died and was raised for them. So we have stopped evaluating others from a human point of view. At one time we thought of Christ merely from a human point of view. How differently we know him now! This means that anyone who belongs to Christ has become a new person. The old life is gone; a new life has begun!*
> (2 Corinthians 5:14–17)

While my old identity changed in a heartbeat, it took some time for my thinking to catch up with this profoundly different objective reality. Yes, various behaviors, such as excessive drinking and stinginess that were inspired by fear of lack, changed almost immediately. It became my burning desire to know God and to follow His leading. However, it took some time for God's declarations concerning my identity as set forth in the Bible, particularly in the New Testament, to replace the old programming that had been instilled by years of autonomous living.

In the investment world that I occupied for decades, it was quite easy to be distracted by urgent matters that demanded my attention.

A company in which our funds invested misses its earnings guidance and the stock plummets. A key employee resigns unexpectedly. Or—fill in the blank. I have discovered that if I'm not mindful of my true identity, it is easy for me to react to circumstances in business (or in life in general) in an inappropriate manner. I confess to forgetting on occasion who I truly am.

The remainder of this chapter covers some of my learnings about identity and how this understanding helps me better represent Jesus in leadership. By continually reminding myself of my true identity, I have found that I am better prepared to navigate the challenges of life, including leading others and responding to crises.

A STUDY IN CONTRASTS

Shortly after I surrendered my life to Jesus, the movie *Chariots of Fire* came to theaters around the world. While the movie is filled with memorable scenes surrounding the events of runners preparing to compete in the 1924 Olympics, those related to the issue of self-worth leap off the screen every time I watch it. The striking difference between two athletes' take on their personal identity is vividly captured in the following movie lines. Reflecting on the upcoming race, Harold Abrahams says, "And now in one hour's time, I will be out there again. I will raise my eyes and look down that corridor—four feet wide, with ten lonely seconds to justify my existence. But will I?" By contrast, Eric Liddell says in a different scene, "I believe God made me for a purpose, but He also made me fast. And when I run, I feel His pleasure."[28]

---

28. *Chariots of Fire*, directed by Hugh Hudson (1981; Warner Bros., USA and Canada; 20th Century Fox, International).

The source of self-worth for these two characters could not have been more different. For Abrahams, his identity was all about himself. By running fast, he hoped to *achieve* his identity through meritorious performance. Liddell's identity was wrapped up in God. Having already *received* his identity based upon Jesus dying for him (God's merit, not his own), he ran fast to give God pleasure.

Liddell continued to live under the knowledge of his true identity well after the 1924 Olympics. He returned to the University of Edinburgh, from which he graduated in 1924 with a Bachelor of Science degree. In 1925, after competing in some athletic events, Liddell returned to China, where he had been born, to serve as a missionary teacher. Except for two furloughs in Scotland, he remained in China. In 1941, when life there became very dangerous because of Japanese aggression, Liddell sent his wife and daughters away to live in Canada while he joined his brother serving the poor in a rural mission station. Ultimately, he was imprisoned in a Japanese civilian internment camp, where he died in 1945. According to a fellow missionary, Eric Liddell's last words were, "It's complete surrender," in reference to how he had given his life to God.[29]

WHAT IS THE SOURCE OF MY IDENTITY?

Based on what they say and do, most business leaders I have met in the corporate world identify themselves in terms of what they do. Like Harold Abrahams, their self-worth is often vested in their position in a corporate hierarchy earned through personal performance. When

29. Sally Magnusson, *The Flying Scotsman, A Biography* (New York: Quartet Books, 1981), 167.

leaders travel, it is not uncommon for them to chat with strangers about what they do. When someone seated next to us on a plane asks what we do, we tend to interpret the question as "Who are you?" After stating our identity in terms of role and responsibilities, we typically reciprocate the question.

This reality begs an important question: do we determine our own identity, or does someone else do that? Is it internally or externally decided? In this regard, it is helpful to define the word *identity*. Identity can be defined as "sameness in all that constitutes the objective reality of a thing."[30] This definition implies that identity is objectively determined externally rather than subjectively determined internally through self-examination. While we are the authors of what we do, we are not the authors of who we are. My parents named me, and that identity has tagged me since birth, regardless of anything I've done. As much as some might want to believe they are the authors of their identity, this idea is nonsensical.

Individuals often attempt to create an identity for themselves in the brave new world of social media. Mark Zuckerberg, cofounder and CEO of Facebook, said, "Think about what people are doing on Facebook today. They're keeping up with their friends and family, but they're also building an image and identity for themselves, which in a sense is their brand."[31] This so-called brand is the inventor's attempt to create a face admired by others.

As a follower of Jesus, I look to God to tell me who I am. After all, it is He who has determined my purpose and, by extension, my

30. "Identity," Merriam-Webster. Accessed March 2, 2021. https://www.merriam-webster.com/dictionary/identity.
31. Fred Vogelstein, "The Wired Interview: Facebook's Mark Zuckerberg." Wired, Conde Nast. Accessed March 2, 2021. https://www.wired.com/2009/06/mark-zuckerberg-speaks/.

identity. He owns me and has placed His brand upon me.[32] This truth guides my approach to life, including all my personal and professional relationships. Having adopted me into His family, God (by His perfect and unchanging nature) will not reverse course. Since I know and am secure in who I am in Him, I am at peace. I am not caught up in the all-too-common search for self-worth. The sure knowledge of who (and whose) I am is the anchor in life's storms that enables me to deal with everything that comes my way.

In the New Testament, there are many passages concerning the believer's identity. However, for the purposes of this chapter, we will focus on the five aspects of our identity cited in the following excerpt from the apostle Peter's letter to the church:

> *But you are a chosen people, a royal priesthood, a holy nation, God's special possession, that you may declare the praises of Him who called you out of darkness into His wonderful light. Once you were not a people, but now you are the people of God; once you had not received mercy, but now you have received mercy.*
> (1 Peter 2:9–10 NIV)

I AM COMPLETELY ACCEPTED

According to the apostle Peter, I have been chosen by God Himself. Every one of us can relate to how special we feel when chosen by someone else. Thinking back to certain competitions in which my

32. Note that a steer does not brand itself! The owner brands the steer.

investment firm engaged, I vividly recall my excitement when the client chose us.

Of course, the eternal God is in a completely different category from that of a prospective client! The all-powerful and all-knowing God chose me despite my many missteps and irrespective of my good (at least in my opinion) performance. Simply put, I am consequential by virtue of Jesus' total acceptance of me.

In his letter to the church at Ephesus, the apostle Paul says, *Even before He made the world, God loved us and chose us in Christ to be holy and without fault in his eyes* (Ephesians 1:4). Think about that! You were on His mind before He created anything. What would your reaction be if someone told you he or she had been thinking about you and praying for you daily for your entire life? Would you be thankful? Would you feel special? Well, God has had you on His mind and in His heart for a lot longer! Based upon this fact alone, you should feel very special!

Your acceptance by God is not anchored in your performance. Rather, it is anchored in the truth that God Himself has made you acceptable. In Paul's letter to Titus, he says, *Because of his grace he [God] made us right in his sight and gave us confidence that we will inherit eternal life* (Titus 3:7). Thankfully, God has accepted me based upon His merit rather than my own. As I reflect on this truth, I am overwhelmed both by how special I am to God and by the permanence of my "accepted" status.

Let's apply this truth in the context of the marketplace. In a sense, all business activity revolves around the goal of gaining the acceptance of the other stakeholders in the businesses we lead. In fact, nothing happens in the world of business without the lubricant of acceptance.

When customers buy our products, they are accepting them and, by extension, are accepting us. When a board of directors accepts our strategic recommendations, they are accepting us since our credibility is integral to the decision. The people who report directly to us work most effectively when they accept us by trusting our leadership. Our shareholders accept our stewardship of the companies we lead when we earn their acceptance through value creation, including growth in earnings per share.

There is nothing inherently wrong with earning the acceptance of others. The concept of trust manifested through acceptance is a necessary precondition to fulfilling the mission of any business. However, if our identity is thoroughly wrapped up in the acceptance of others, we might be motivated to do whatever it takes to gain or retain acceptance. The actions prompted by the drive for acceptance can undermine our witness for Jesus and can sometimes end very badly. I am reminded of the tragic case of Enron Corporation. Once a darling of the business world, Enron collapsed one day because the senior leadership, driven by the need to meet the expectations of shareholders, published misleading financial information. The accounting fraud was exposed, and the company filed for bankruptcy, dragging down shareholders, thousands of employees, and some key service providers along with it.

As followers of Jesus, we cannot engage in unethical practices, for doing so would dishonor God. However, we can still undermine our effectiveness as leaders if our identity as leaders is so wrapped up in the acceptance of others that we forget who we truly are, which informs why we exist in the first place. By constantly focusing on the truth that we are totally and unconditionally accepted by our Creator (the most important stakeholder in our lives), we can retain a healthy perspective on who we are, including the fact that God's acceptance of us is unconditional, despite our imperfections and mistakes. It will never be revoked.

I AM EXTREMELY VALUABLE

Not only are followers of Jesus accepted, but we are also extraordinarily valuable. Peter describes believers as a holy nation, God's special possession. In Paul's letter to the church at Corinth, he provides additional color regarding the concept of God's ownership: *You have been bought and paid for by Christ, so you belong to Him* (1 Corinthians 7:23 TLB).

The cost incurred when we purchase anything can be quite different from its market value from time to time. The market value is based upon the price an independent (arm's-length) party is prepared to pay. Decades ago, Mary and I paid a certain price to purchase a house in a very nice neighborhood. The cost was highly relevant to us since we had to take out a large mortgage loan to close the purchase. Unfortunately, we needed to sell after the huge meltdown in the real estate market in the early 1990s. As a result, the price we received was about 75 percent of what we had paid, and the net to us after repaying the mortgage loan was less than 60 percent of what we had invested. Our cost was irrelevant to the buyer.

Similarly, we might spend large sums acquiring a higher education, but at the end of the day, our "market value" is what employers are prepared to pay for our services. While the compensation offered might be influenced by our education and, by extension, how much we paid for it, our value in the market will be whatever prospective employers are prepared to pay us.

In this context, it is instructive to consider how much God paid for us. This value was established by Jesus, who died on our behalf to reconcile us to God. It is a price beyond comprehension. The measure of Jesus' selfless act cannot be quantified. Having led a life of perfect obedience to God the Father and being completely innocent of any crime, He accepted the punishment we deserve for all our crimes against God and our fellow human beings—past, present, and future.

Because it is by God's grace we are saved, one could say that the cost of our good works is entirely irrelevant to our value. Unlike the real estate market, the value God places on each of us doesn't fluctuate based upon His mood or our failures. It follows that, notwithstanding contrarian messages from others or from your own self-assessment, you are valuable beyond measure in this life and throughout eternity.

In the business world, we can easily slip into the habit of valuing ourselves based upon performance and performance-based rewards. For example, let's say that the bonus you receive this year is not up to your expectations. Whatever the explanation, your value as a person is unaffected. The value of what you did might have declined in the opinion of the person to whom you're accountable, but your value as a person accepted by God is infinite and unchanging. The opposite scenario is equally true. A larger-than-expected bonus should not lead us to be arrogant, but rather humble. After all, we didn't get to where we are solely by ourselves.

As a corollary, when we are secure in our true value, we are more aware than ever of the value of every person we meet since everyone is made in the image of God. In the realm of commerce, this truth encompasses the lives of all stakeholders in our companies, including our employees, customers, shareholders, suppliers, and service providers. When we see everyone as valuable to God, we are better equipped to represent Him well to them. External circumstances might affect our economic value (at least in the short term), but they do not affect our true value.

I AM ETERNALLY LOVED

One of the best-known verses in the Bible is John 3:16: *For God so loved the world that he gave his one and only Son, that whoever believes in him shall not perish but have eternal life* (NIV). A deep understanding of the fact that God considers us lovable (as Peter says, we are God's *special possession*) is essential to an accurate perception of our identity. It is one thing to comprehend this truth intellectually, but it is quite another thing to know it at the heart level. By that, I am referring to a revelation of truth that comes from the spiritual rather than the intellectual realm.

An excellent example of head versus heart knowledge occurred on a mission trip a few years ago. For more than two decades, Mary and I have traveled to several different nations as part of a teaching team. The curriculum was developed by our home church to help leaders grow in their leadership role. On one of these trips, our team was in Ghana teaching a group of about five hundred pastors and other leaders from across the country. On the second day, we focused on God's love for each of them. Most of the attendees were well versed in the Bible and, more specifically, in what the New Testament has to say about God's love. In all likelihood, every one of them could have recited John 3:16 verbatim. Their *head knowledge* of God's love was rock solid.

At the end of that day, we invited them to come forward for prayer. Men prayed for men and women prayed for women. I felt led to hug each of the men filing by, in some cases saying a short prayer. The following day, one of the conference organizers excitedly called me over. He introduced me to a pastor who proceeded to thank me profusely for my prayer the previous day.

Prior to arriving for the conference, this pastor decided that his marriage was dead. As a result, he planned to file for divorce immediately following the conference. He told me that for the previous twenty years, he had not once told his wife he loved her. None of his children were married, for they did not like what they saw in their parents' marriage. When I hugged him the previous day, however, he said that he suddenly got a *heart revelation* of the magnitude of God's love for him. Overwhelmed by this love, he walked through the door of his home that evening, told his wife he loved her, and asked her to forgive him for his mistreatment of her. At the same conference the following year, we saw him and his wife together. They confirmed that their marriage was fully restored and the family stronger than ever—all because of the heart revelation of God's amazing love.

It is impossible to truly love others or ourselves without a clear revelation of God's love for us. After all, God is love. It is one of His eternal attributes. The apostle John says, *We love each other because he loved us first* (1 John 4:19). Not only does God's love affect how we treat others in the marketplace, but it also affects how we think of ourselves. Business can be tough. Tempers sometimes flare and things are said that have the potential to hurt. If we are secure in God's love, however, we can weather verbal attacks and respond as God would want us to.

I AM TOTALLY FORGIVEN

Forgiveness is the hallmark of the Christian worldview. When we choose to accept the message of the cross, we admit that we are sinners in need of forgiveness. By trusting in Jesus' finished work on the cross, we acquire a fresh new identity—children of God. Our heavenly passport is stamped "Forgiven!" About this truth, the apostle Peter wrote, *Once you had not received mercy, but now you have received mercy* (1 Peter 2:10 NIV), while the apostle Paul said, *There is now no condemnation for those who are in Christ Jesus* (Romans 8:1 NIV).

I can lose sight of the truth that I am totally forgiven, even though it is an integral part of my identity. While I easily give mental assent to the fact of forgiveness, I do not always act like I believe it. It is sometimes difficult to shake free of self-denunciation when I make mistakes. In fact, it is sometimes difficult to forgive myself, even though the clear message of the New Testament is that God has completely forgiven me. Therefore, I must regularly remind myself that I am totally forgiven, and I must meditate on the enormous price Jesus paid to win my forgiveness. As the apostle Paul said, *He is so rich in kindness and grace that he purchased our freedom with the blood of his Son and forgave our sins* (Ephesians 1:7). The more deeply I comprehend the magnitude of what God has done for me, the more this truth moves from my head to my heart.

Importantly, the more deeply I internalize this truth, the more easily I forgive and ask forgiveness from others. I recall one occasion when I was confronted by an upset colleague. I had visited a large institutional investor whom my colleague had introduced to our firm, and he strongly felt that I should have asked him to go along on the call. I suspect he expected me to respond with an aggressive justification of my action. Instead, I apologized on the spot since I concluded that he was in the right and I was in the wrong. Noticeably surprised, he accepted my apology, and that was the end of the matter. I should add that I was the CEO but chose not to play that card! Just because we might occupy a senior position in the corporate hierarchy does not give us licence to avoid seeking forgiveness. Humility demands it.

I AM FULLY CAPABLE

According to the apostle Peter, all believers (including marketplace leaders) are called to the priestly responsibility of doing God's work and speaking out for Him. *The Message* paraphrases it this way: *But you are the ones chosen by God, chosen for the high calling of priestly work, chosen to be a holy people, God's instruments to do his work and speak out for him, to tell others of the night-and-day difference he made for you* (1 Peter 2:9). We will discuss the implications of the priestly dimension of a marketplace leader's calling later in the book, but for now, let's focus on the issue of capability.

Would God choose us to fulfill a priestly function without equipping us to handle the assignment? Such an assertion is preposterous, for it is contrary to God's nature. The New Testament makes it very clear that God Himself equips us with the capacity to fulfill this specific calling. Referring to himself in his second letter to the Corinthian believers, the apostle Paul says, *Not that we are competent in ourselves* to claim anything for ourselves, but our competence comes from God (2 Corinthians 3:5 NIV). This competence is not something external to us that we must call down when necessary or spend years in a seminary developing.

Rather, it is internalized the moment we trust in Jesus—because God the Holy Spirit comes to dwell inside every believer.[33] Paul wrote, *I have been crucified with Christ and I no longer live, but Christ lives in me* (Galatians 2:20 NIV). Elsewhere, Paul writes, *I can do all things through Christ who strengthens me* (Philippians 4:13 NKJV). The reality is that the same Holy Spirit who indwelt the great apostle Paul indwells every follower of Jesus. For this reason, we are fully capable of fulfilling our priestly calling.

A strong internalization of our true identity is essential to fulfilling God's call on us as marketplace leaders. It is also necessary to enable us to be authentic in all our marketplace activities, which means that everything we think, say, and do should be informed by our true identity as followers of Jesus. In short, we are completely accepted, extremely valuable, eternally loved, totally forgiven, and fully capable as ministers of the new covenant.

WAKE-UP CALL

Do you see yourself as more than your business card? In your marketplace role, do you think of yourself as a person made by God in His image? Do others respond to you as a title or as God's ambassador? Do you tend to define yourself in terms of what you do and what you

---

33. See Romans 8:10; 2 Corinthians 4:6–7; Galatians 1:15–16; Galatians 2:20; Galatians 4:19; Ephesians 3:17; Colossians 1:27; and 2 Thessalonians 1:10.

achieve in the marketplace? Have you fully grasped that it is God, not your employer, who determines your identity, and that you receive that new identity when you trust in Jesus? Finally, are you so deeply aware of your God-determined identity that it spills out of you in whatever situation you find yourself?

PART 3:
CALLED TO KNOW

WHAT SHOULD I KNOW WHEN FOLLOWING JESUS IN THE MARKETPLACE?

Chapter 6

KNOW JESUS!

Now this is eternal life: that they know you,
the only true God, and Jesus Christ,
whom you have sent.

—JESUS (JOHN 17:3 NIV)

When I first encountered Jesus, I knew virtually nothing about Him in the sense of head knowledge. In that moment, however, I knew Him *relationally*. I surrendered my life to Him, and He placed His Holy Spirit in me. While I had not heard many Bible verses, I knew Jesus by the witness of His indwelling Holy Spirit. Given my general propensity to intellectualize issues, I find it interesting (if not humorous) that God bypassed my intellect completely when He revealed Himself to me.

Nicky Gumbel, vicar of Holy Trinity Brompton and developer of the Alpha Course, points out that there is a huge difference between whom you know and what you know:

> There are also different types of knowledge, and they are not all equally valuable. In French, there are two different words for "to know." One (*savoir*) means to know a fact, the other (*connaître*) means to know a person. God is more interested in us knowing people than facts. The most important knowledge of all is knowing God and being known by Him.[34]

The foregoing brings to mind a personal scenario that played out many times when we lived in downtown Toronto. During my frequent walks to the office, I often engaged with people living on the edge who, not surprisingly, asked for a handout. On many such occasions, I struck up a conversation during which I asked if they knew Jesus. In every single case I can recall, they said yes. When they did, I clarified that I was not asking if they knew *about* Jesus, but rather, I wanted to know if they actually knew Him. At that point, most admitted they did not!

There is a distinction between spiritual revelation and intellectual knowledge. On the one hand, the Bible makes it clear that since God is Spirit, knowing Him necessitates a spiritual encounter. On the other hand, God gave us a mind and intended for us to use it. Some people have doctorates in theology and know a lot about God, but if they don't have a personal relationship with Jesus, they have missed the whole point of the incarnation! In fact, some unschooled evangelists have greatly impacted the society of their time. The apostle Peter, who had a very rudimentary education, is a great example of this.

Assuming we had a genuine encounter with Jesus, how can we

34. Nicky Gumbel, August 12, 2020 (Bible in One Year, 2020), Bibleinoneyear.org.

know Him better both as a person and in terms of what He accomplished? The Bible, which is the inspired word of God, is the means by which we get to know Jesus better (see 2 Timothy 3:16–17). While the experience of God's presence is very important, what we believe about Him must be consistent with what the Bible says. For this reason, I have read the Bible almost every day since first meeting Jesus. I do my best to ensure that any professional or personal decision is anchored in the Bible's teaching.

KNOW WHO GOD IS

God is the Creator. While most people in the West today are biblically illiterate, a large percentage are familiar with the very first verse of the Bible: *In the beginning God created the heavens and the earth* (Genesis 1:1). This verse is pregnant with information concerning some important attributes about the God of the Christian worldview.

First, He is the Creator of everything that came to be, which in the Hebrew rendering is "the heavens and the earth." Second, "in the beginning" implies there was a start to everything and that He is also the creator of time itself (the temporal domain), which progresses unidirectionally forward from that finite beginning. The profound implication of these few words in the Genesis account is that God created all of space, time, energy, and matter. By definition, this means that God is incomprehensibly powerful, or in theological terminology, omnipotent. Since God is the cause of creation, He is not part of it. He is the uncaused cause who is invisible and immaterial. He dwells in an uncreated non-temporal realm called eternity that has existed forever.

In his book *The God Delusion*, atheist Richard Dawkins presents an argument against Christian claims that he thinks is strong, if not irrefutable. Based upon the premise that every physical effect has a cause, Dawkins asks what caused God. In taking this approach, he consciously or unconsciously redefines the Christian God as part of the created order. However, in the words of Dr. John Lennox, Emeritus Professor of Mathematics at the University of Oxford, the God of the Bible is the author of the "whole show," not a part of it.[35] As the uncaused cause, He is eternally self-existent.

God is personal. Another important attribute of the biblical God is that He is personal, having a mind, a consciousness, and a desire for relationship with humankind. This personal attribute is in sharp contradistinction to some impersonal force. His personality is revealed throughout the Bible as He communicates with and acts in the lives of humankind, in particular the Jewish people, and, supremely, in the person of Jesus Christ.

Another extension of His personal nature is His purposefulness. This attribute implies that everything, including us, has been created for a purpose. Consistent with this notion of purpose, astrophysicists have determined that the universe has been finely tuned to a virtually incomprehensible degree (see chapter 9). Stated differently, the evidence for design is everywhere, including many different physical constants that have only been discovered in recent decades. Without such fine-tuning, life in general and human life in particular would be impossible. It should be added that wherever we see design, we automatically infer that it is the product of mind rather than of random

35. John Lennox, "Not the God of the Gaps, but the Whole Show," The Times, 17 Aug. 2012, www.thetimes.co.uk/article/not-the-god-of-the-gaps-but-the-whole-show-hc6zn90zkrt.

forces. Moreover, these scientific discoveries accord with the Christian worldview that God created everything with humanity in mind.

Many scientists of a materialist persuasion acknowledge the presence of design but attempt to escape the obvious implication of a designer by referencing the appearance of design rather than the reality of design. For example, Richard Dawkins wrote, "Biology is the study of complicated things that give the appearance of having been designed for a purpose."[36] The motive behind these mental gymnastics would seem to be a philosophical bias against the biblical account of creation, a point transparently articulated by Professor Richard Lewontin, a geneticist, as follows:

> It is not that the methods and institutions of science somehow compel us to accept a material explanation of the phenomenal world, but, on the contrary, that we are forced by our a priori adherence to material causes to create an apparatus of investigation and a set of concepts that produce material explanations, no matter how counter-intuitive, no matter how mystifying to the uninitiated. Moreover, that materialism is absolute, for we cannot allow a Divine Foot in the door.[37]

Note that Lewontin's objection to a designer is philosophical rather than scientific.

God is perfect in all His ways. The adjective *perfect* means "having all the required or desirable elements, qualities, or characteristics; as

36. Richard Dawkins, *The Blind Watchmaker* (London: Penguin Books, 1986), 1.
37. Richard C. Lewontin, "Billions and Billions of Demons," The New York Review of Books, August 27, 2020. https://www.nybooks.com/articles/1997/01/09/billions-and-billions-of-demons/.

good as it is possible to be."[38] Regarding *good*, Jesus on one occasion responded to a young man's question by saying, *Why do you call Me good? No one is good but One, that is, God* (Mark 10:18 NKJV). Jesus is saying that only one being is perfect, and that Being is God. His answer echoes an assertion in the Old Testament text that *God's way is perfect* (2 Samuel 22:31; Psalm 18:30).

This latter text relates to God's moral perfection, which includes numerous qualities attributed to Him in the Bible. In his classic work *The Knowledge of the Holy*, A.W. Tozer explores several of these attributes (all of which illustrate His perfection) in some detail. For now, I simply want to identify and comment briefly upon a few. Please note that God is not an aggregation of attributes. Rather, He is fully every one of His attributes everywhere, at all times, and to everyone. According to Tozer, "Because [God] is a unity He never suspends one of His attributes to exercise another."[39]

God is immutable. According to Tozer, this means He "never differs from Himself."[40] Put another way, His character attributes never change—not even one iota! By contrast, I simply have to look inward! On occasion, I can be inconsistent and illogical. I can also change my mind. Hopefully, such changes are based upon new information, but they could also be driven by less than perfect motives. This amazing truth concerning God's immutability lends absolute stability, reliability, and trustworthiness to all His other attributes.

God is omniscient. God knows everything. He even knows my secret thoughts! Unlike me, He is not dealing with a lack of data.

---

38. "Perfect," Lexico Dictionaries. Accessed March 2, 2021. https://www.lexico.com/en/definition/perfect.

39. A.W. Tozer, *Knowledge of the Holy* (San Francisco, CA: Harper One, 2009), 98.

40. Ibid., 53.

This attribute implies that He is never surprised by new information that might cause us fallible human beings to stumble or change course. Taken together with the biblical assertion that God is love, His all-knowing nature creates the possibility of deep intimacy between humankind and God.

God is all-wise. Wise means "marked by deep understanding, keen discernment, and a capacity for sound judgment," and also "possessing inside information."[41] Wisdom is marked by the ability to assess the data at hand and use it to form sound judgments. Since God knows our every thought, He possesses all inside and outside information. Fully informed by all the facts and shaped by perfect understanding, discernment, and judgment, His wisdom is morally perfect.

God is love. God's love for us can be characterized as His infinite goodwill toward each one of us. This goodwill implies that God bears us no malice or evil intent. Rather, God is friendly toward us and always has our very best interests in mind since we are the objects of His love. Amazingly, His love is unconditional; therefore, it is not subject to our doing anything to earn it. Neither is it disqualified by our misdeeds. He demonstrated His love by dying for us even though we are unworthy of His sacrifice (see Romans 5:8).

God is just. Always fully love, God is simultaneously always fully just. True love requires true justice, and true justice requires true love. The word *just* means "acting or being in conformity with what is morally upright or good."[42] It implies the meting out of appropriate penalties for wrongdoing. In the Christian worldview, justice will ultimately

41. "Wise," Merriam-Webster. Accessed March 2, 2021. https://www.merriam-webster.com/dictionary/wise.
42. "Just," Merriam-Webster. Accessed March 2, 2021. https://www.merriam-webster.com/dictionary/just.

be served since death is not the end. According to the Bible, there will be a final judgment when Jesus will judge every person with justice.

God is holy. Holy means "exalted or worthy of complete devotion as one perfect in goodness and righteousness."[43] When applied to the God of the Bible, the word *holy* is a weak container for expressing its full meaning. According to Tozer, "We know nothing like the divine holiness. It stands apart, unique, unapproachable, incomprehensible, and unattainable."[44] Because of His holiness, God cannot abide the very presence of evil. The prophet Isaiah catches a glimpse of God's holiness and is completely undone by the revelation of his own uncleanness (sinfulness) in God's presence (see Isaiah 6:1–5). At that moment, the prophet articulates humanity's fundamental problem.

God is sovereign. God's sovereignty can be defined as His "absolute right to do all things according to His good pleasure."[45] As the Creator, God is the supreme authority and therefore has the right to hold human beings accountable for their actions in accordance with His perfect justice.

God is triune. When I was quite young, my parents compelled me to attend church regularly, although none of it really stuck until I was in my mid-thirties! However, I recall that the congregation of my parents' church in Vancouver, Canada, sang the hymn "Holy, Holy, Holy" in every service. This hymn, which includes the words "God in three persons, blessed Trinity," neatly captures the mystery of one God (unity) in three persons (trinity). The three persons of the Trinity

43. "Holy," Merriam-Webster. Accessed March 2, 2021. https://www.merriam-webster.com/dictionary/holy.
44. "Tozer Devotional: God's Holiness Is Unique," The Alliance. Accessed March 2, 2021. https://www.cmalliance.org/devotions/tozer?id=1422.
45. "Sovereignty," Easton's Bible Dictionary. Accessed March 2, 2021. https://eastonsbibledictionary.org/3487-Sovereignty.php.

are the Father, Son, and Holy Spirit. While distinct, these three persons are coeternal and identical in substance and nature at all times. Christians know this to be true based on biblical revelation; the historical evidence of Jesus' life, death, and resurrection; and the experience of life according to the Holy Spirit. For centuries, followers of Jesus have subscribed to the doctrine of one God in three persons as formulated by the early church fathers in the Nicene Creed. The triune nature of God underpins the truths that God is both love and relational since these attributes require more than one person to operate.

KNOW WHAT GOD ACCOMPLISHED THROUGH JESUS CHRIST

Houston, we have a problem! According to the Genesis account, humanity lost its intimate relationship with the Creator due to sin. Because of humanity's broken nature since the original couple's treasonous rebellion, humanity's default setting became self-determination. In the twenty-first century, this is still the key problem. Not only was paradise lost when the first couple sinned, but death became the new omnipresent, unchangeable reality. Over the millennia, different cultures have invented various religions to address these two problems. Alternatively, some worldviews, like atheism, deny these problems altogether; or like Hinduism and Buddhism, they focus on the solution of different problems based upon their theories about the nature of reality.

The Bible makes it very clear that we cannot, by our own efforts, achieve or even facilitate reconciliation with God. The reason is simple. Imagine that every wrong thought, word, or deed you have ever had or committed is a liability. Imagine further that a description of each misdeed has been written down and compiled under the label "debt owed to God." As a former corporate banker, I am not particularly worried about debts owed by a company that has sufficient cash in its bank accounts to fully repay the debt. By simply transferring cash in the amount owed to the lender, the borrower fulfills its legal obligation and the debt is marked "paid in full."

This analogy breaks down, however, when applied to our indebtedness to God. The problem is twofold. First, our good deeds are actually not virtuous from God's perspective. According to the Bible, *all our righteous acts are like filthy rags* (Isaiah 64:6 NIV). Any good deeds we do, no matter the magnitude, are never good enough to satisfy God's holy requirements. Even if an objective assessment of the good deed based upon its positive impact scores it high marks, God looks at the heart and, in particular, our motives. Regarding our hearts, the Bible says, *The heart is deceitful above all things and beyond cure* (Jeremiah 17:9 NIV). Bearing in mind that God knows our every thought and motivation, even when we don't, we can begin to appreciate that none of our good deeds can possibly offset even the tiniest misdeed.

Second, as previously discussed, God is infinitely good. By contrast, our smallest misdeed (for example, that "little white lie") is infinitely bad. Over the course of our lives, this debt that cannot be repaid grows continuously. Since it cannot be repaid and since it represents a lifetime accumulation of the injustices we have committed, God, by His holy nature, must render justice. According to His warning in the garden of Eden, the penalty for any such violation is eternal, spiritual death. That means, among other things, eternal conscious separation from the Creator God in a realm called hell. Some might consider such a judgment to be unfair, but if we remember that God created us in His image and for His purposes, it seems only reasonable that He would hold us accountable to His standards. He has the perfect sense of justice, even if it does not seem to meet our human, finite definition of justice and fairness.

Only God can solve our problem. Amazingly, God stepped into our broken world and dealt with the one problem we are absolutely powerless to solve. Out of His infinite love for each one of us and in accordance with Old Testament prophecy (see appendix A), God entered history in the person of Jesus Christ two millennia ago. This clear biblical assertion is a mystery beyond human comprehension. However, the Bible affirms Jesus as being both fully human and fully divine. Like us in our humanity, He was subject to normal human pressures, including temptation and the need for food and rest. Also, His human nature was subject to death, as demonstrated on the cross. Unlike us, Jesus was, is, and always will be the eternal Son of God. Together with the persons of God the Father and God the Holy Spirit, He was co-architect and co-creator of the universe. One of the Gospel accounts says, *He [Jesus] was with God in the beginning. Through Him all things were made; without Him nothing was made that has been made* (John 1:2–3 NIV).

Throughout His earthly ministry, Jesus lived in unbroken communion with God the Father, even while He daily interacted with sinful (and often hostile) people. He never once sinned. Lest we skip over this assertion too quickly, try to imagine a single day in your entire life when your every motive, thought, word, and deed were 100 percent perfect. Exactly! Jesus' every motive, thought, word, and deed were perfect over a period of about twelve thousand days. In doing so,

Jesus completely fulfilled the requirements of the Mosaic law without the need to offer sacrifices for His own wrongdoing.

Jesus' singular goal was to lay down His life as a sacrifice for humanity's sin by bearing in His sinless body God's justified wrath against all human wrongdoing—past, present, and future. We could say that Jesus was literally born to die. He chose to lay down His life on our behalf. Recall the words of John the Baptist: *Look! The Lamb of God who takes away the sin of the world!* (John 1:29). Under the Mosaic law, the people of God lived under a covenant with Him in which sins were covered through the sacrifice of unblemished animals to atone for wrongdoing. This old covenant foreshadowed the new covenant in which Jesus, the perfect Lamb of God, bore our punishment. The new covenant put into effect by Jesus rendered the old covenant obsolete.

Approaching the problem from another perspective, we are not sinners because we sin; rather, we sin because we are sinners. Our identity is based upon who we are rather than what we have done. Therefore, we must take on a new identity that has been reconciled with God through Jesus' atoning sacrifice. As discussed in chapter 5, when we personally trust in Jesus, we become that new creation. The old person (our old identity) dies, and a new person and a new identity are born. In theological terms, the righteousness of Jesus Christ is imputed to us when we surrender to Him. In this way, we are made right with God. The debt we owe has been paid in full!

We cannot earn our salvation. Rather, we are forgiven and reconciled with Him through God's grace. Paul, in his letter to the church in Ephesus, puts it this way:

God saved you by His grace [unmerited favor] when

you believed. And you can't take credit for this; it is a
gift from God. Salvation is not a reward for the good
things we have done, so none of us can boast about
it. For we are God's masterpiece. He has created us
anew in Christ Jesus, so we can do the good things He
planned for us long ago. (Ephesians 2:8–10)

Note that God's plan for Christians includes good works, not to earn His favor, but in gratitude for His unfathomable mercy.

What's the catch? Reflecting my investment background, the skeptic in me always surfaces whenever I hear an outrageously attractive offer. If it seems too good to be true, it probably is—right? God's offer of forgiveness, reconciliation, and eternal life based on no effort on my part seems far, far too good to be true!

However, there is a very real catch to this offer. In order to activate the benefits, we must do something very difficult. We must admit in our hearts that we are sinners in need of forgiveness. Put differently, before trusting in Jesus' work on the cross, you, I, and *everyone* continuously asserts personal lordship over their own lives. In order to receive God's gracious gift of forgiveness, we must admit our sin, admit our own wrongdoing and fallen state, and ask for His forgiveness, surrendering our autonomy in favor of His rule over our lives. For most people, this particular exercise of free will is a very tall order!

The Bible refers to this act of surrender as repentance, which means a total change of mind. It is not simply giving mental assent to the existence of God. Rather, with His help, I aim to live for Him as my Creator and the primary One to whom I am accountable. For most of us, the admission of personal guilt and our inability to control our destiny runs counter to human pride. Our natural inclination is to assert control.

To clarify, surrender does not mean that we never again engage in ungodly conduct after putting Him in charge. Unfortunately, we will all continue to sin and fall short after we surrender to Christ. However, the motivation behind my desire to make matters right changed the instant I surrendered to Jesus. Prior to becoming a believer, I generally shrugged off misdeeds (including their negative consequences) as simply a normal part of the human condition. As a follower of Jesus, however, my primary motivation is to make matters right with God and those I may have hurt, irrespective of the personal consequences.

My motivation now comes from gratefulness for what He has done for me and His command to love Him and other people. The Bible says that by virtue of being in relationship with God, I have been set free from the power of sin. It no longer controls me as it once did. Instead, as a child of God, I am led by the Spirit of God who now lives in me.

WAKE-UP CALL

You are likely already a believer in Jesus. However, perhaps you think your Christianity is based solely upon your own good works, such as regular church attendance, knowledge of the Bible, or involvement in various worthy charitable endeavors. The key question for you is this: do you actually know Jesus, or do you simply know about Him?

If you don't yet know Jesus, now is your opportunity. According to John's Gospel, knowing Jesus is the very definition of eternal life (see John 17:3).[46]

46. Appendix B explains how you can begin the most fulfilling chapter of your life by becoming a follower of Jesus.

Chapter 7

KNOW THAT THE BIBLE IS TRUSTWORTHY

*All Scripture is inspired by God and is useful to
teach us what is true and to make us realize what
is wrong in our lives. It corrects us when we are
wrong and teaches us to do what is right.*

—THE APOSTLE PAUL (2 TIMOTHY 3:16)

Knowing Jesus secures our identity as God's children. The Bible, particularly the New Testament, is the cornerstone that supports our knowing Him, including His will for our lives. Christian orthodoxy is based entirely upon the claim that the Bible, while written by human agents, is God-breathed—hence the common label of "Holy Bible."

Echoing Paul's instruction to his student Timothy, the apostle Peter proclaimed, *Above all, you must realize that no prophecy in Scripture ever came from the prophet's own understanding, or from human initiative. No, those prophets were moved by the Holy Spirit, and they spoke from God*

(2 Peter 1:20–21). Since God, being perfect, does not lie, the Bible is inerrant. However, in light of antipathy to the Christian worldview in many cultures today, believers must be absolutely confident in the Bible's trustworthiness.

For many non-Christians, particularly those who have received a higher education, the claim that the Bible is true is often rejected out of hand, greeted with mockery, or both. Sadly, this opinion is almost never based upon a careful examination of the case for the Bible's reliability. Critical thinking is generally not the foundation of most opinions these days. Instead, many people dismiss the reliability of the Bible based upon the almost exalted status of the scientific enterprise.

In chapter 9, we will explore the perceived conflict between science and the Christian worldview. Spoiler alert: they are not mutually exclusive. In the West in particular, many people erroneously assume that science can answer every question, and therefore they think that the Bible is irrelevant. Unfortunately, most young people today often parrot what they are taught without giving it much thought. This is arguably not their fault. After all, the naturalist worldviews of most of those who teach them are often conveyed as absolute truth. Can we realistically expect them to criticize the views of these authority figures?

The case for the trustworthiness of the Bible is based upon the answers to two major questions: Is the Bible we have today an accurate translation of the original handwritten manuscripts? If the answer to that question is yes, then is the Bible true?

IS TODAY'S BIBLE AN ACCURATE TRANSLATION OF THE ORIGINAL MANUSCRIPTS

The question regarding the accuracy of today's Bible when compared to the original manuscripts (aka autographs) can be broken down into two distinct sub-questions. First, are the handwritten manuscripts we have today accurate copies of the autographs? Second, are the translations into other languages from these copied manuscripts accurate?

Regarding the original language manuscripts, the Bible stands alone from all other ancient literary works in terms of the sheer number of manuscripts discovered to date. For example, there are more than five thousand manuscripts written in the Greek language alone, in addition to thousands more in other languages, including Hebrew and Aramaic. Importantly, most manuscripts are only portions of Scripture—in some cases as little as a few words. While manuscripts exist in several different languages, the majority of scholarly focus is on Greek manuscripts of the New Testament since the expert consensus is that the autographs were written in Greek.

When studying these ancient manuscripts, scholars known as textual critics identify differences (variants) between the various manuscripts. Their goal is to unearth what the original authors (as opposed to the copyists) actually wrote. Most importantly, they want to determine whether the differences among these copied manuscripts undermine any core doctrines that underlie the Christian worldview.

One of the most influential textual critics today is Bart Ehrman, who at one time claimed to be a Christian, but today describes himself as an agnostic. One of his most famous books is *Misquoting Jesus*, which attempts to shock readers into sharing his conclusion that the

Bible we have today is based upon an enormous number of scribal errors in the manuscripts. Untrained readers might well find his analysis unsettling, particularly if they hold the Bible in high regard. Yet toward the end of the book, Ehrman admits that "of all the hundreds of thousands of textual changes found among our manuscripts, most of them are completely insignificant, immaterial, of no real importance for anything other than showing that scribes could not spell or keep focused any better than the rest of us."[47] Therefore, based upon Ehrman's own words, we can have confidence in scholarly opinion as to the content of the autographs. The very few larger passages that remain subject to dispute are well known and are properly footnoted in any good Bible.[48] None affects any core doctrine.

Regarding the question of translation from the original language into the so-called target languages like English or French, we rely on committees of scholars who are well-versed in both the original languages and the target languages. Different translations adopt different translation philosophies. For example, the New King James Version and the English Standard Version are considered word-for-word translations that attempt to preserve the form of the original language, and as a result, they sometimes do not flow smoothly. By contrast, the New International Version is based upon a thought-to-thought approach whereby the translators attempt to capture the original thought behind the manuscript text as opposed to the original language structure of the texts. As a result, it tends to be easier to read.

While many Christians have strong feelings about which is the best translation, it is my opinion that all three versions mentioned

47. Bart Ehrman, *Misquoting Jesus: The story behind who changed the Bible and why* (New York, HarperOne, 2007), 207.
48. For example, see John 7:53–8:11 concerning the woman taken in adultery.

above are good translations upon which to rest one's beliefs. When reading any version of the Bible, my practice is to pray that the Holy Spirit will help me to understand what God is saying to me at that moment. After all, the Holy Spirit, being the very essence of truth, can lead us into all truth!

IS THE BIBLE TRUE?

Assuming that the Bible we hold is an accurate translation of the autographs, is the original true? Before plunging into several lines of evidence that persuade me that the Bible is true (i.e., trustworthy), an overview of this remarkable book is in order.

It is fair to say that the Bible is utterly unique in the annals of literature. It is essentially a compilation of sixty-six different books (thirty-nine in the Old Testament and twenty-seven in the New Testament). It was written by many different authors over a period of about fifteen hundred years, including a gap of about four hundred years between the Old Testament (OT) and the New Testament (NT) during which no writings were contributed to the Bible.

While most of its human authors are identified within the Bible or by tradition, some are not. It is generally agreed that the total number of different authors is around forty, most of whom were Jews (including those who wrote the New Testament). The writings include several different literary genres, including historical narratives, Gospels (biographies of Jesus), poetry, wisdom literature, and letters.

Most importantly, as seen in the earlier quoted words of Paul and Peter, the Bible claims that its ultimate author is God the Holy Spirit! In other words, every word of the Bible is co-authored by the writer and the Holy Spirit. As a result, the various books sometimes reflect differences of style and emphasis based upon the writer's perspective and background, but the books are unified under the supervision of the Holy Spirit. This biblical claim of supernatural co-authorship is unique in literature, and it is the reason believers reverently refer to the Bible as the Word of God.

Notwithstanding the different genres, the enormous time span over which the books of the Bible were written, and the large number of different authors, the Bible displays an astonishing degree of coherence. Christians believe that the metanarrative, or big picture, knitting the books of the Bible together is God's unfolding plan to rescue humankind from the consequences of sin, thereby enabling a relationship with the Creator. This plan was fully unveiled in Jesus Christ, the Son of God.

Some people have explained the thematic integrity of all sixty-six books of the Bible by describing the New Testament as concealed in the Old Testament and the Old Testament as revealed in the New Testament. The metanarrative flows from:

1. God's creation of the universe, culminating in His creation of the first couple, to

2. the rebellion of the first couple, resulting in their estrangement from God, to

3. His election of a specific people (the Jews) to whom He initially revealed Himself and through whom He would, in the fullness of time, bring the Messiah to reconcile all of humankind (not just the Jews) to Himself, to

4. the history of the Jews as they attempted (and largely failed) to follow His commands, to

5. the arrival of the Messiah promised in the Hebrew Scriptures, to

6. the death and resurrection of the Messiah, to

7. the history of the early church, and finally, to

8. the second coming of Jesus Christ and the final judgment of humankind.

Therefore, there is an underlying unity behind the multifaceted diversity found within the biblical text.

LINES OF EVIDENCE SUPPORTING THE TRUTH CLAIMS OF THE BIBLE

For purposes of this discussion, I will cover six lines of evidence:

1. The manuscripts we have were written relatively soon following the events recorded.

2. They were based upon eyewitness accounts.

3. The eyewitnesses often died while refusing to recant their testimony that the accounts were true.

4. Many details in the NT accounts would have been embarrassing to the leaders of the early church.

5. Many of the NT accounts fulfilled prophetic utterances given centuries earlier.

6. Extrabiblical writings support the historicity of the Bible, as do many archaeological discoveries.

With the exception of points five and six, these evidences focus on the reliability of the New Testament.

EARLY DATING OF THE NEW TESTAMENT BOOKS

An important aspect in determining whether writings accurately reflect the events they claim to record is when they were written relative to the dates of the events. As the gap of time increases, myth tends to creep into accounts, making it difficult to uncover what, if anything, in the account actually occurred versus embellishments and pure fabrication. As it happens, the books of the New Testament were written relatively soon after the events they record.

In Paul's letter to the church in Corinth, he makes the following statement:

> *For what I received I passed on to you as of first importance: that Christ died for our sins according to the Scriptures, that he was buried, that he was raised on the third day according to the Scriptures, and that he appeared to Cephas, and then to the Twelve. After that, he appeared to more than five hundred of the brothers and sisters at the same time, most of whom are still living, though some have fallen asleep. Then he appeared to James, then to all the apostles, and last of all he appeared to me also, as to one abnormally born.* (1 Corinthians 15:3–8 NIV)

Scholars generally agree that in this passage, Paul is citing a creedal statement that had been circulating among believers since the resurrection, probably a gap of less than five years following the event. Note that it captures the core of historic Christianity, including the fact of Christ's death, the purpose of His death, His burial, His resurrection on the third day, and His physical appearance to a large number of people—including Peter, James, and Paul himself. While there continues to be debate regarding the precise date of when each book was written, there is no serious debate concerning their early authorship.

It is significant that not one of the Gospel accounts or letters makes reference to one of the most significant events in the history of Israel—namely, the total destruction of Jerusalem and the temple by the Roman army in AD 70. Given the devastating impact on the Jewish nation, including the elimination of the Jews' means of reconciliation to God through temple sacrifice and the dispersal of the Jewish people throughout the ancient world, one would have expected some reference. The reasonable inference is that all the Gospels and letters were written prior to AD 70.

EYEWITNESS TESTIMONY

In law, the importance of eyewitness testimony is central to uncovering whether allegations are true. If the person providing evidence is one or more steps removed from the eyewitness being cited, the testimony is hearsay and is much less credible. Most of us have played the "broken telephone" game where the message mutates rapidly as it gets passed along from one mouth to another. The final message is often quite different from the original. The reason relates to human fallibility. People often don't listen carefully, or they paraphrase according to their own communication style. Sometimes they deliberately alter the message for their own reasons. In any event, in the realm of evidence, eyewitness accounts by credible witnesses are the best way of determining the truth.

Applying this concept to the Gospel accounts and the epistles, one could say they are the evidential gold standard. With the exception of Luke, all are eyewitness accounts by individuals who encountered the risen Jesus and, in many cases, spent years with Him during His earthly ministry. To cite just one example, the apostle John makes the following statement:

> *That which was from the beginning, which we have heard, which we have seen with our eyes, which we have looked at and our hands have touched— this we proclaim concerning the Word of life. The life appeared; we have seen it and testify to it, and we proclaim to you the eternal life, which was with the Father and has appeared to us. We proclaim to you what we have seen and heard, so that you also may have fellowship with us. And our fellowship is with the Father and with his Son, Jesus Christ.* (1 John 1:1–3 NIV)

Notice all the references to firsthand physical contact with Jesus, including seeing, hearing, and touching Him.

MOST EYEWITNESSES REFUSED TO RECANT THEIR TESTIMONY, AND THEY DIED AS A RESULT

Over the course of history, many people have subscribed to philosophies and have died believing they were true; therefore, their sacrifice had merit. For example, based upon the Qur'an and other original sources, many Islamists believe that a martyr's death earns them paradise. In the religious component of the Islamic ideology, the certainty of this reward is very significant. Unlike the God of the Bible, Allah of the Qur'an does not necessarily keep promises. He is described as the best of deceivers (see Qur'an 3:54). As a result, a Muslim cannot know with certainty that he or she is destined for paradise. The exception is death through martyrdom (see Qur'an 22:58–59).

By contrast, I have never heard of someone dying willingly for a cause they knew to be false. That brings us to the apostles. A major reason for the persecution they endured, even martyrdom, was their insistence that they had seen the risen Christ. If they had just conjured up the resurrection as a part of their religious narrative, surely they would have recanted when faced with death for their false belief. After all, who would die for a cause they knew to be a lie?

EMBARRASSING CONTENT IN THE NEW TESTAMENT

The human tendency is to avoid transparency since it relates to a person's own weaknesses and misconduct. Either we avoid any reference to our mistakes or we provide versions of events that are favorable to us.

In this context, it is relevant that the New Testament accounts are full of details that would have been very embarrassing to the apostles. The early church leaders are often presented as slow to comprehend Jesus' clear teaching on many topics, including the nature of the kingdom of God, His impending death at the hands of the authorities, and His resurrection on the third day after His death. On one occasion, after Peter told Jesus that His death at the hands of men would never happen, *Jesus turned and said to Peter, "Get behind me, Satan! You are a stumbling block to me; you do not have in mind the concerns of God, but merely human concerns"* (Matthew 16:23 NIV). No one would proudly record this account of failure, but someone interested in telling the truth would.

Jesus rebuked some of them for calling for the death of their enemies, as well as thinking only of themselves, as when John and James competed for the seats of honor next to Jesus in His coming kingdom. All the men abandoned Him at the time of His arrest, and most went into hiding. After vehemently promising Jesus that he would never deny Him, Peter did so three times within twenty-four hours!

Moreover, the women were the real heroes at the time of Jesus' death and resurrection. They stayed by Him during His crucifixion and were the ones who discovered the empty tomb. In the culture of that day, a woman's testimony carried little, if any, weight and was treated as unreliable when compared with that of a man. Yet the women and their testimonies play a significant role in the Gospel biographies. Given most leaders' tendency to present matters in the most favorable light to themselves, the only reasonable explanation is that the accounts are true. They record what really happened, warts and all.

NEW TESTAMENT FULFILLMENT OF OLD TESTAMENT PROPHECY

Appendix A provides an overview of Jesus' fulfillment of Old Testament prophecy. In a nutshell, Jesus perfectly fulfilled dozens of Old Testament prophecies that were recorded hundreds of years before His incarnation. Given the number of different prophets and the time span separating them from the predicted events, this fact is amazing and points to the truth of the biblical accounts. Mathematicians have estimated the probability of these many different prophecies being fulfilled in one person, and it is close to the square root of zero! The New Testament writers saw Jesus' fulfillment of Old Testament prophecy as proof of His identity as the Jewish Messiah and Savior of the world.

EXTRABIBLICAL SUPPORT OF THE BIBLICAL NARRATIVES

There are numerous ancient writings outside of the Bible, as well as archaeological discoveries, that support the biblical narratives. None of them prove that the Bible is true, but they are consistent with the biblical accounts.

For example, Josephus, the respected Jewish historian, wrote about Jesus. In his *Antiquities of the Jews*, he wrote:

> Now, there was about this time Jesus, a wise man, if it be lawful to call him a man, for he was a doer of wonderful works—a teacher of such men as receive the truth with pleasure. He drew over to him both many of the Jews, and many of the Gentiles. He was [the] Christ; and when Pilate, at the suggestion of the principal men among us, had condemned him to the cross, those that loved him at the first did not forsake him, for he appeared to them alive again the third day, as the divine prophets had foretold these and ten thousand other wonderful things concerning him; and the tribe of Christians, so named from him, are not extinct at this day.[49]

49. *Josephus, The Complete Works: The Antiquities of the Jews,* translated by William Whiston (Nashville; Thomas Nelson, Inc., 1998), 576.

While not a follower of Jesus, Josephus records many details about Jesus and the early church as history. Without exception, his historical commentary accords with the books of the New Testament.

Modern archaeology has uncovered numerous artifacts that support the biblical record. At one time, many critics viewed the biblical accounts as myth and fabrication since there was no archaeological evidence supporting many of the names, places, and practices at that time. Fast-forward to the twenty-first century. There have been numerous discoveries verifying many of the figures referenced in the Gospels, particularly from Luke's biography. Sir William Ramsay, one of the world's greatest archaeologists, said, "Luke is a historian of the first rank; not merely are his statements of fact trustworthy, [but] he is possessed of the true historic sense. . . . In short, this author should be placed along with the greatest of historians."[50]

With knowledge that the Bible is trustworthy, we will now explore how Scripture supports the reliability of the resurrection account, the lack of conflict between science and faith in God, and the reliability of the truth claims of the Christian worldview versus those of other worldviews. While I have encountered other objections to the Christian worldview over the years, these are the ones that come up most frequently, especially among those in leadership.

My treatment of these objections is far from exhaustive, particularly in light of the vast amount of scholarly research and writing on each topic. At the end of this book, there is a bibliography to assist anyone interested in gaining more insight on the various questions covered in this book.

50. Sir William Ramsay, *The Bearing of Recent Discovery on the Trustworthiness of the New Testament* (London: Hodder and Stoughton, 1915).

WAKE-UP CALL

Do you feel uncomfortable referring to the Bible? Are you concerned that your peers might consider you a religious fanatic? Are you worried that you would lose credibility with your peers if you mention something from Jesus' teachings? Be encouraged by the foregoing evidence that supports the trustworthiness of the Bible. You are on solid ground when you base your beliefs and actions on Scripture.

Here is a challenge. The next time you are traveling somewhere by plane or train, openly read your Bible. People around you will notice what you are reading, and that could spark some exciting conversations!

Chapter 8

KNOW THAT THE RESURRECTION OF JESUS IS ROOTED IN HISTORY

*For if the dead are not raised, then Christ has
not been raised either. And if Christ has not been
raised, your faith is futile; you are still in your sins.
Then those also who have fallen asleep in Christ
are lost. If only for this life we have hope in Christ,
we are of all people most to be pitied.*

—THE APOSTLE PAUL
(1 CORINTHIANS 15:16-19 NIV)

My faith in Jesus began when He declared to me, "I am alive." While my encounter was spiritual rather than physical, I immediately accepted the clear physical implication of these three little words. Jesus Christ was raised from the dead. However, many people today consider the resurrection story to be just that—a story. They certainly think it is a nice story, but they think it is a fictional account. Even some who claim to be followers of Jesus think of the resurrection account as a story to be taken allegorically. For example, they might view it as symbolizing the hope that God the Creator will take us to be with Him in some spiritual sense when we die.

Many dismiss a physical resurrection out of hand since, according to their worldview, miracles are impossible. Based upon naturalism, their worldview excludes the supernatural and confines reality exclusively to the physical realm. Since the claim that Jesus was raised from the dead falls in the category of a miracle, the naturalist presupposition precludes the possibility of a physical resurrection.

Even if non-believers know someone who claims to have experienced a divine healing, they reason that other physical factors explain it rather than God's intervention. Finally, and not uncommonly, many dismiss the notion of Jesus' resurrection because they do not like its implications. For example, if Jesus' resurrection is true, it supports the assertion that the Bible is true, which in turn supports the assertion that we are all ultimately accountable to God.

But what if it is true? Many non-believers from various backgrounds and fields of expertise have attempted to disprove the resurrection. They have rightly concluded that if they can disprove this purported event, then the Christian worldview falls apart since, as the apostle Paul explains, it rests entirely on the truth of Jesus' physical resurrection. The truth of the resurrection is not a sidebar to Christianity, but it is the centerpiece. In any event, after thoroughly investigating this claim, many of these well-educated skeptics turned around 180 degrees and became followers of Jesus.

From leading an investment company, I learned (sometimes the hard way) the importance of explicitly identifying key assumptions and assessing their validity prior to making any investment decision. On occasion, our team discovered that we had been proceeding toward a positive decision while unaware of one or more key hidden assumptions we were making. If these assumptions were untrue, then the probability of writing off the investment completely was unacceptably large.

Similarly, one who holds naturalism to be true is investing her or his entire life in a worldview based on a philosophical assumption that is unprovable. Given this reality, a critical thinker should be open to considering competing hypotheses. If a naturalist's worldview is untrue and Christianity is true, the loss for the naturalist will not only affect their physical life but also their afterlife, which stretches throughout eternity.

The principle of basing conclusions on evidence as opposed to philosophical presuppositions applies when one examines a historical hypothesis. Since the resurrection is a historical claim, it cannot be adjudicated in the courts of science. Rather, it must be adjudicated in the courts of history.

In the case of the generally agreed facts concerning Jesus' death, burial, and resurrection, Christians throughout the centuries have believed that the best explanation is that Jesus was raised from the dead. They would strongly disagree with the atheist philosopher Nietzsche, who asserted that believers in Jesus abandoned reason in favor of an irrational hope.

The Christian worldview is solidly anchored in reason that is based upon historical evidence. It is interesting to note that many highly regarded scientists, such as Dr. Ian Hutchinson, professor of nuclear science and engineering at MIT, unashamedly proclaim their belief in the resurrection based on a close examination of the facts.[51] It is indisputable, in light of his professional training, that Hutchinson is far more knowledgeable about the physical realm than was Nietzsche, yet Hutchinson is a Christian and Nietzsche was not. Pondering this one fact should cause anyone to open their mind to objectively examine the evidence.

Let's begin to examine that evidence. We will first look at the implications of the claim that Jesus was raised from the dead. Then we will consider generally accepted historical facts surrounding Jesus' death, burial, and post-mortem appearances. Finally, we will consider the explanatory power of the resurrection hypothesis versus competing hypotheses to assess which one best fits the facts. This approach to explaining phenomena is called inference to the best explanation. It is used in various fields of study, including any scientific realm where one cannot test the hypothesis in a laboratory (such as, for example, the origin of the universe).

IMPLICATIONS OF THE CLAIM THAT JESUS WAS RAISED FROM THE DEAD

Several years ago, I regularly went to a barber named Ali. While he came from a Muslim background, Ali wasn't a particularly observant Muslim. He either was not well versed in the ideology of Islam or, if so, didn't live by it. In any event, I often spoke with him about my faith in Jesus and challenged him to consider becoming a follower of Jesus. On one occasion, we discussed the resurrection of Jesus and

51. Ian Hutchinson, "Can a Scientist Believe in the Resurrection? Three Hypotheses," The Veritas Forum, June 1, 2017. http://www.veritas.org/can-scientist-believe-resurrection-three-hypotheses/.

the evidence in favor of it.[52] At the end of our conversation, I asked Ali what his reaction would be if he were to become persuaded that Jesus was in fact raised from the dead. His response was immediate and unambiguous: "I would have to pay attention to Jesus!" I couldn't have said it better than Ali! He intuitively understood the world-shaking implications of the resurrection. It is by far the most important event in all of human history.

Many people do not consider its implications, however, since they assume the resurrection claim is untrue. If it is true, though, its implications are extraordinary. For followers of Jesus in the marketplace, these implications should bolster our confidence in Jesus and in the biblical record.

THE RESURRECTION VALIDATES JESUS' CLAIM OF DIVINITY

In the four Gospel accounts, Jesus consistently asserted or implied His divinity. For example, in John's Gospel, He said, *The Father [God the Father] and I are one* (John 10:30). While Jesus never explicitly says, "I am God" in the New Testament, He often used phrases that, to the Jewish mind of that time, clearly meant the same thing. These included the phrases "Son of God," "Son of Man," and "I Am." He called God His Father, which to the religious leaders was blasphemous since it equated Him with God.

Jesus also did not correct His disciples when they called Him the

---

52. One of the reasons I concluded that Ali was not well versed in the religious claims of Islam is that he didn't raise the normal Muslim objection to the resurrection claim. According to Islam (which thinks highly of Jesus as a sinless, miracle-working prophet), Jesus did not die on a cross, and therefore the physical resurrection is irrelevant and is a significant error in the Christian Scriptures.

Messiah. He affirmed Peter's assertion that He was *the Messiah, the Son of the living God* (Matthew 16:16). However, these claims (or at least their implications) apparently went over the heads of His followers at the time. They hung on His every word, but they failed to comprehend when He told them He would die and be raised back to life on the third day.

Jesus held the crowd's attention with the many miracles He performed, the authority with which He spoke, and the compassion with which He treated the people who came to Him. He did not stop people when they worshiped Him. Think about that for a moment! Based on their Scriptures, the Jews were strict monotheists. In their worldview, the worship of anyone other than God was blasphemy, and, according to their law, the death penalty applied. Ultimately, the religious authorities condemned Jesus to death for precisely that reason. At His trial, many charges were brought against Him, but none stuck due to lack of evidence.

Finally, as recorded in the Gospel of Matthew, the following interaction took place between the high priest and Jesus:

> *And the high priest arose and said to Him, "Do You answer nothing? What is it these men testify against You?" But Jesus kept silent. And the high priest answered and said to Him, "I put You under oath by the living God: Tell us if You are the Christ, the Son of God!" Jesus said to him, "It is as you said. Nevertheless, I say to you, hereafter you will see the Son of Man sitting at the right hand of the Power, and coming on the clouds of heaven." Then the high priest tore*

his clothes, saying, "He has spoken blasphemy! What
further need do we have of witnesses? Look, now
you have heard His blasphemy! What do you think?"
They answered and said, "He is deserving of death."
(Matthew 26:62–66 NKJV)

If Jesus was raised from the dead, everything He said prior to the crucifixion is validated, including His claim to divinity. After all, death is the common denominator affecting everyone, yet Jesus overcame death—something that can be reasonably attributed only to an unimaginably powerful, invisible force like God. As my friend Ali said, if the resurrection is true, everyone should pay close attention to everything Jesus said. In particular, we should pay attention to Jesus' assertions concerning His divinity, the meaning of His crucifixion, and the unconditional offer of forgiveness that opens the door to reconciliation with God. All these claims should logically command the attention of a critical thinker.

THE RESURRECTION VALIDATES THE TRUTH OF THE BIBLE

In chapter 6, we addressed various objections to the trustworthiness of the Bible. However, if Jesus was in fact raised from the dead, then we are not limited solely to the very strong historical case for the accuracy of the Bible. We have God incarnate declaring it to be true!

On several occasions, Jesus told those around Him that the biblical accounts were true. Of course, when He walked on the earth, the Bible was what we now refer to as the Old Testament. The New Testament was written after His earthly ministry. Among other things,

He said that the Scripture *cannot be broken* (John 10:35 NKJV), it is *the word of God* (Mark 7:13), and it is indestructible (Matthew 5:18). Moreover, when interacting with the people of His day, Jesus regularly referred to Old Testament accounts, such as David's actions, the destruction of Sodom, Cain's murder of Abel, and the calling of Moses. Therefore, if a person claims to believe in Jesus, they should also believe the Old Testament accounts since the Son of God believed in the value of the Old Testament and viewed it as authoritative.

THE RESURRECTION VALIDATES PROPHECIES CONCERNING THE FUTURE MESSIAH

As seen in appendix A, Jesus fulfilled many Old Testament prophecies. Among other things, these prophecies can be seen (with the clarity of hindsight) as looking ahead to His death, burial, and resurrection. That is why Jesus often connected prophetic utterances with Himself. The apostle Paul frequently connected Jesus' resurrection with Old Testament Scriptures. In a way, we could say that the Old Testament prophecies validate Jesus' identity and claims, and Jesus' resurrection validates Old Testament prophecies.

THE RESURRECTION MEANS THAT I, TOO, WILL BE RESURRECTED!

The Bible asserts that all believers in Jesus will at some future time be resurrected from the dead. Since Jesus validated all the Bible's claims by being raised from the dead, followers of Jesus can take the promise of their personal resurrection to the bank!

Given the pressures of life, I often lose sight of this specific promise, but when I take time to think about it, I am deeply encouraged. Like Jesus after the resurrection, I will no longer experience bodily weakness, pain, sickness, or sorrow. Moreover, in my new body, I cannot die again because God has determined I will live with Him throughout eternity. This hope of the resurrection propelled the early church to live passionately for Christ without fearing negative consequences.

WHAT ARE THE AGREED-UPON HISTORICAL FACTS CONCERNING THE RESURRECTION NARRATIVE?

In the investment management business, most analyses of the investment outlook include both top-down and bottom-up elements. A top-down approach considers broader economic and financial market trends to determine their implications in terms of asset mix in an investment portfolio. A bottom-up approach considers individual companies and their investment merit based upon their specific strategies and resources in the context of broader economic and financial market trends.

In the case of the claim that Jesus rose from the dead, this top-down/bottom-up analogy can be applied. By "top down," I mean that believers accept the Bible as the inspired Word of God, along with its clear affirmation that Jesus was raised from the dead. They do not feel the need to carefully analyze the strength of the historical case for Christ. In any event, most people lack the training or the time to engage in such an analysis. For believers down through the centuries, the top-down approach has been sufficient for most people who, like me, have had a genuine encounter with Jesus and have surrendered to His leadership.

The bottom-up approach considers the question of the resurrection using accepted analytical techniques for studying history, such as the critical historical methodology. It is not assumed that the Bible is inspired by God. Rather, all the data, both biblical and extra-biblical, is looked at through a historical lens. The goal is to tease out significant facts that are overwhelmingly agreed upon by properly trained scholars. Such scholars typically teach in a university setting, and their various publications are subjected to peer review. This scholarly approach is unbiased since input is welcomed from a wide ideological spectrum within the academy that ranges from atheism to agnosticism to liberal Christianity to conservative Christianity.

From this point, we will take the bottom-up approach by examining some major facts that are overwhelmingly agreed upon within the academic community. It should be noted that this strong consensus is a relatively recent development. Not that long ago, scholars would have vigorously argued over and disputed most of the facts discussed herein. There were some who even questioned the historicity of Jesus' existence, although virtually no serious scholar today would entertain such a notion. For those of us who are Christians, these facts strongly support the Christian belief that Jesus was raised from the dead. However, if we simply treat that belief as one hypothesis among several, the task becomes to determine which of the competing hypotheses best supports the agreed-upon evidence.

For purposes of this exercise, I sought and received permission from Dr. William Lane Craig to reproduce in its entirety an article he wrote concerning the resurrection. It can be found in appendix C. Craig holds a PhD in philosophy from the University of Birmingham and a Doctor of Theology degree from the University of Munich. The title of his doctoral thesis that he wrote while at the University of Munich is *The Historical Argument for the Resurrection of Jesus During the Deist Controversy (1985)*. He has authored or edited more than thirty books and has had almost two hundred articles published in professional and theological journals. In addition, Craig has debated many of the world's most prominent atheists, including Sam Harris, Lawrence Krauss, Sir Roger Penrose, and the late Christopher Hitchens.

As you will see, the arguments underpinning the historicity of the resurrection are compelling. That is a very good thing for two distinct reasons. One, as followers of Jesus, we are required to believe that the physical resurrection actually occurred (see Romans 10:9). Two, as the apostle Paul stated (see 1 Corinthians 15:14–17), if it did not occur, our faith is futile!

The implications of Jesus' physical resurrection from the dead are stunning. They include the validation of (1) Jesus' claim to divinity, (2) the truth of the Hebrew Scriptures contained in the Old Testament, (3) the truth of prophecies concerning the future Messiah, and (4) my hope that I, too, will one day be physically resurrected like Jesus. Implications 1–3 are anchored in historical facts agreed upon by most scholars today. The hypothesis that Jesus was raised from the dead fits the agreed-upon historical facts much better than any other hypothesis that has ever been advanced.

When asked about his reaction if he were to become convinced of Jesus' physical resurrection, Ali, my former barber, said, "I would have to pay attention to Jesus!" If your peers were to become convinced that Jesus was actually raised from the dead, what do you think they might do?

WAKE-UP CALL

Is the resurrection a topic you avoid when speaking about your faith in God? Does it embarrass you? Can you see that a robust response regarding the truth of the resurrection can open the door to deeper conversations about your faith in God? After all, the implications are profound!

Chapter 9

KNOW THAT FAITH IN GOD IS COMPATIBLE WITH MODERN SCIENCE

Men became scientific because they expected
Law in Nature, and they expected Law in Nature
because they believed in a Legislator.

–C. S. LEWIS

Stephen Hawking, a world-famous scientist, died in March 2018. Besides being a formidable intellect, Hawking was a profile in courage. He owed one part of his fame to his triumph over amyotrophic lateral sclerosis (aka Lou Gehrig's disease). For more than fifty years, he defied the normally fatal condition and pursued a brilliant career that amazed doctors and his many fans around the world.

Hawking was one of the most influential scientists of the modern era. Therefore, when he pronounced several years ago that "because there is a law of gravity, the universe can and will create itself out of nothing," some saw it as the final word on the non-existence of God.[53] He suggested in his writings that true knowledge is accessible only through the scientific enterprise. In doing so, he pronounced philosophy dead—to the undoubted surprise and consternation of his professorial colleagues who worked in the various faculties outside the physical sciences.[54]

Is Hawking correct? Is science the ultimate arbiter of truth? While I am not a scientist, I have studied both science and this topic extensively. With all due respect to Hawking's scientific prowess, my studies have led me to the conclusion that his assertion is wrong. Ironically, his declaration that philosophy is dead is a statement of philosophy, not of science. Some people who are not followers of Jesus, however, lean on Hawking's scientific credibility to dismiss the concept of faith in God out of hand rather than to personally engage in critical thinking.

On the flip side of the coin, many followers of Jesus are uncomfortable with the science-faith debate. They feel out of their depth. As a result, they sometimes privatize their faith to avoid exposing their ignorance on this issue. This is a tragedy in light of Jesus' command to share our faith in Him with others. Also, the apostle Peter exhorted us to always be prepared to defend our faith (see 1 Peter 3:15). In the remainder of this chapter, we will explore the following big questions:

53. Stephen Hawking and Leonard Mlodinow, *The Grand Design* (New York, NY: Bantam, 2012), 180.
54. From *The Grand Design*, by Stephen Hawking and Leonard Mlodinow: "Traditionally these [the big 'why' questions of life] are questions for philosophy, but philosophy is dead. It has not kept up with modern developments in science, particularly physics. As a result, scientists have become the bearers of the torch of discovery in our quest for knowledge."

1. Is there a conflict between science and faith in God?
2. Are there limitations to science?
3. Do the latest findings of science lend credibility to the claim that God exists?

IS THERE A CONFLICT BETWEEN SCIENCE AND FAITH IN GOD?

As capably articulated by Dr. John Lennox in his book *Gunning for God: Why the New Atheists Are Missing the Target*,[55] there are excellent reasons to believe that the domains of science and faith in God are neither mutually exclusive nor in conflict. However, many people believe that science and faith in God are incompatible for various reasons. As previously mentioned, one reason is an unwillingness to engage in critical thinking. Another is science's enormous success in uncovering the mechanisms underpinning the physical world. This exponentially expanding body of knowledge has birthed rapid technological advances that, in turn, have elevated the status of the scientific enterprise in the public mind.

Perhaps most importantly, many young people today are the products of schools and universities that teach that the two domains contradict one another. Invoking the philosophical Law of Noncontradiction, the proponents of this view argue that one side must be true and the other false. Given the authority and perceived expertise of their professors, it is easy to understand why young people might be reluctant to confront them with opposing viewpoints.

55. John C. Lennox, *Gunning for God: Why the New Atheists Are Missing the Target* (Oxford, England: Lion Hudson, 2011).

Since many academics today would subscribe to Hawking's assertion about the extraordinary explanatory power of science, they convey their opinion as truth rather than as opinion. It doesn't help that Christians are often mocked for their unwillingness to abandon their faith in God in favor of facts unearthed by science. Such mockery is common not only in the academic world but also in the media and Hollywood.

The first sentence of the Bible says, *In the beginning God created the heavens and the earth.* Prior to the mid-twentieth century, scientists generally believed that the universe was eternal. In doing so, they explicitly disagreed with the biblical account. When strong evidence arose that the universe emerged in the finite past, many scientists initially resisted this conclusion because it gave credence to the biblical account. Among the deniers was Albert Einstein, who found most disagreeable the fact that his general theory of relativity implied a beginning. As a result, he manipulated his equations by inserting a cosmological constant to align his theory with the hypothesis of an eternal universe. However, based upon evidence for a beginning produced by other scientists, including Edwin Hubble (of Hubble Telescope fame), Einstein is alleged to have admitted that his cosmological constant was his biggest blunder. As a result, he eliminated it. Today, there is an overwhelming scientific consensus that the universe had its beginning in finite time.

Though it is common for non-believers to pit science and faith against one another—Richard Dawkins has labeled Christians "faith heads," saying that attributing the creation of the universe to God is due to giving up when something is too hard to understand scientifically—it is easy to prove there is no conflict whatsoever between science and faith in God.[56] Simply put, many scientists throughout the centuries to the present day were passionate about both science and their belief in God. For example, Sir Isaac Newton, a scientist and Christian theologian, is widely recognized as one of the most influential scientists of all time. Other famous scientists who professed their Christian faith and played an important role in the modern scientific revolution include Robert Boyle, Francis Bacon, and Johannes Kepler.

According to a review of Nobel prizes awarded between 1901 and 2000, 65.4 percent of Nobel Prize laureates have identified Christianity in its various forms as their religious preference. Overall, scientists identifying as Christians have won a total of 72.5 percent of all the Nobel Prizes in Chemistry, 65.3 percent in Physics, and 62 percent in Medicine.[57] However, according to American writer and philosopher Robert M. Pirsig, "When one person suffers from a delusion, it is called insanity. When many people suffer from a delusion, it is called Religion."[58, 59]

Are we to believe that all these eminent scientists are deluded? Obviously not. Common sense tells us that the theory of a conflict between the two domains is falsified by the reality that a great many scientists are Christians. The two camps differ in their respective worldviews but not in their scientific profession. In the words of Dr.

56. Richard Dawkins, *The God Delusion* (Boston: Houghton Mifflin Co., 2006), 13.
57. Baruch Aba Shalev, *100 Years of Nobel Prizes* (Los Angeles: The Americas Group, 2003).
58. As quoted by Richard Dawkins, *The God Delusion* (Boston: Houghton Mifflin Co., 2006), 28.
59. "*The God Delusion* makes me embarrassed to be an atheist, and the McGraths [co-authors of *The Dawkins Delusion*] show why."—Michael Ruse, Atheistic Philosopher.

John C. Lennox, Emeritus Professor of Mathematics, University of Oxford, "Not all statements by scientists are statements of science."[60]

Several years ago, a very gifted doctor performed video-assisted thoracic surgery to remove a cancerous tumor from my right lung. I was very thankful to him and his team, and at the same time, I found a greater appreciation for God's creative genius in making our world intelligible. Anticipating order, scientists discovered regularities in nature from which they formulated testable theories. As one result, we have skilled doctors today who use advanced technology to perform delicate, lifesaving surgeries. For me, there is absolutely no need to choose between science and faith in God. The scientific enterprise is one dimension of God's providence.

ARE THERE LIMITATIONS TO SCIENCE?

If there is no logical requirement to choose between science and faith in God, are there natural limitations on the explanatory scope of the physical sciences? There is no doubt that science has been amazingly successful in helping us understand how the material universe works. These discoveries have fueled great technological leaps forward. Science cannot, however, answer some of the most basic questions posed by my grandchildren! This reality implies that the scope of science is limited. Sir Peter Medawar, biologist and Nobel laureate, puts it this way: "The existence of a limit to science is, however, made clear by its inability to answer childlike elementary questions having to do with first and last things, questions such as How did everything begin? What are we all here for? What is the point of living?"[61]

60. John C. Lennox, *God and Stephen Hawking* (Oxford: Lion Hudson, 2011), 14.
61. John C. Lennox, *God and Stephen Hawking* (Oxford: Lion Hudson, 2011), 20.

Of relevance to this question, there are many things we all take for granted, even though we do not actually know what they are. Christians are frequently attacked for believing in things they cannot see. However, there are a number of phenomena that science acknowledges as true yet does not know what they are! In other words, we cannot see them. These include gravity, electricity, and consciousness. While scientists admit these exist and have developed theories to explain how they work, they cannot define them other than in regularities or laws that describe how they act (for example, the law of gravity). This enormous and seemingly insurmountable knowledge gap does not lead them or us to throw out the entire realm of science, nor should it lead us to dismiss the possibility of God's existence.

Medawar's perspective notwithstanding, the late Stephen Hawking promoted the view that physics rather than God was the source of ultimate truth. As I reflect on these matters, I am reminded once again that I did not become a follower of Jesus as a result of logic and intellectual reasoning. The question that launched my spiritual journey when I was in my thirties was along the lines of what my purpose was in life. As Medawar noted, this is a childlike, elementary question that cannot possibly be answered by science. In fact, every person I know who, like me, has become a follower of Jesus later in life has done so as a result of a personal revelation of Jesus rather than intellectual reasoning.

I do not mean to downplay the importance of applying our God-given intellect to life's big questions. In fact, I have become a student of the immense intellectual foundation that undergirds the Christian faith. However, when I reflect on why I have put my trust in Jesus, the reason that dwarfs all others is quite simply that I know Him!

His presence in my life is so real that I cannot imagine living without Him. Having said that, there are times when I lose sight of, or (dare I say it?) override, His direction. It is humbling and wonderful to know that His ardent love for me is unaffected when my response to Him is unloving.

DO THE LATEST FINDINGS OF SCIENCE LEND CREDIBILITY TO THE CLAIM THAT GOD EXISTS?

> *They know the truth about God because he has made it obvious to them. For ever since the world was created, people have seen the earth and sky. Through everything God made, they can clearly see his invisible qualities—his eternal power and divine nature. So they have no excuse for not knowing God.*
>
> –THE APOSTLE PAUL (ROMANS 1:19-20)

Almost twenty centuries ago, the apostle Paul penned the above words to the church at Rome. He made it clear that regardless of what people might think or say, they are without excuse when they deny the truth of God's existence since He has made it obvious.

But does Paul's assertion still hold true today? After all, science has unearthed knowledge about the physical realm that was completely unknown to Paul or the people of his day. Do the massive strides in scientific discovery eliminate or make less probable the hypothesis that God is the ultimate explanation behind everything—or do these scientific advances make His existence even more obvious than it might have been to the people in Paul's day? Are people living in the twenty-first century even more without excuse than those living back then?

EVIDENCE FROM COSMOLOGY

Cosmology is the science of the origin and development of the universe. As previously noted, until quite recently the consensus of those not holding a Christian worldview was that the universe has always existed. If one has an eternal landscape upon which to paint hypotheses, it is possible to develop many theories that are difficult to dispute. After all, eternity is a long, long time, and who can possibly know what might have happened in the infinite past?

For example, in working with an eternal canvas, one can claim there is infinite time available to produce everything by chance, including the multiplicity of animal and plant species that currently exist. However, the eternal-universe bubble burst in the early twentieth century as scientists found more and more compelling evidence that the universe came into existence in the finite past. Today, the overwhelming scientific consensus is that the universe sprang into existence billions of years ago from nothing. While some scientists have twisted themselves in knots attempting to show that something can come from nothing, they inevitably propose "nothings" such as quantum vacuums that are, in fact, "somethings." This conclusion concerning the origin of the universe in the finite past has been dubbed the "big bang theory." One moment there was nothing, and the next moment a universe was expanding at breakneck speed.

Science is at a loss to explain this event. Moreover, astrophysicists have determined that the initial conditions governing the four fundamental forces—gravity, the electromagnetic force, and the "weak" and "strong" nuclear forces—were determined less than one-millionth of a second after the big bang and were fine-tuned in such a way that if the ratio among them were off by even an infinitesimal amount, stars could not have formed and there would have been no universe at all!

Scientists have now determined there are more than two hundred parameters fine-tuned to permit the existence of life. If any one of them were altered by even one iota, life could not exist. Such fine-tuning defies any explanations that are based on pure chance. The explanations appear to be purposeful, whereas chance is random and does not operate with an end in mind. The only explanation behind purposeful design is a mind—intelligence—because it is our common experience that design implies a designer. Based on this evidence alone, it would appear that humankind today has less excuse than people had back in Paul's day when he declared that God's power and divine nature were clearly evident to everyone.

On December 25, 2014, the op-ed "Science Increasingly Makes the Case for God," written by Eric Metaxas, was published in the *Wall Street Journal*. In 2015, Metaxas reported that the article had garnered more than six hundred thousand Facebook shares and more than 9,250 comments, making it, unofficially, the most popular article in *Wall Street Journal* history up to that time. Since the piece does an excellent job addressing this question, I sought and received permission from the *Wall Street Journal* and Eric Metaxas to quote the op-ed in its entirety. It can be found at the back of this book in appendix D.

EVIDENCE FROM BIOLOGY

As pointed out, the probability of a universe containing any planets conducive to life, let alone a universe existing at all as a result of purely materialistic causes, is mind-bogglingly infinitesimal. Therefore, the fine-tuning of a universe that is conducive to life points to the existence of a cause outside the universe itself.

The fine-tuned universe does not, however, explain the origin of life. But can this same macro- or cosmological-level argument concerning the likelihood of a transcendent cause be made at the micro or biological level? Note that this question of biological origins splits into two discrete queries. First, how did life arise from non-life in the first place? Second, how did the myriad life-forms around us arise?

Regarding the first question, Charles Darwin, the author of *On the Origin of Species*, admitted he did not have an answer. His starting point assumed the existence of primitive, single-celled organisms, and he proceeded from there. As it happens, Darwin had no idea of the sheer complexity of a single cell. In particular, he had no knowledge of DNA and its information-bearing properties. He simply posited a materialistic theory based upon chance, the passage of time, and survival of the fittest.

Since Darwin's time, scientists have attempted to apply his theory of evolution to explain the development of life from non-life, sometimes referred to as chemical evolution. According to many scientists who regularly attend international symposia concerning the origin of life, this entire field of scientific endeavor has hit a brick wall. Paradoxically, it seems that the more scientists learn about physical reality, the more formidable are the obstacles to understanding life's origin from purely materialistic causes. Indeed, it is the view of Dr. James Tour, a synthetic organic chemist and world leader in the area of nanotechnology, that no one can explain or even conceptualize how life can emerge from non-life.[62] On the other hand, the Bible answers that question with the assertion that life began as the work of the Creator. As God is not part of His creation, we could say that we are a miracle!

Returning to the issue of complex life evolving from less complex ancestors, Darwin admitted that his theory flew in the face of huge gaps in the fossil record, particularly the sudden appearance of new life forms in the Cambrian explosion.[63] He assumed, however, that the fossil record would ultimately yield vast numbers of intermediate animal forms confirming descent from common ancestry (the so-called tree of life still found in most biology textbooks). However, it has not. With the passage of time, the fossil record has become more problematic as additional examples of new creatures suddenly appearing in the fossil record are discovered.

In disciplines that study events in the remote past, theories cannot be tested in laboratories through experimentation and observation. Recognizing this constraint, Charles Darwin and his close friend geologist Charles Lyell articulated a forensic or historical approach for testing scientific theories. According to this method, multiple competing hypotheses are developed to explain a particular phenomenon. The task is to then determine which hypothesis best explains

62. Dr. James M. Tour is the T. T. and W. F. Chao Professor of Chemistry, Professor of Materials Science and NanoEngineering, and Professor of Computer Science at Rice University, Houston, Texas.
63. According to Wikipedia, the Cambrian explosion "was an event approximately 541 million years ago in the Cambrian period when practically all major animal phyla started appearing in the fossil record. . . . Almost all present-day animal phyla appeared during this period." https://en.wikipedia.org/wiki/Cambrian_explosion.

the observed effects. Using this approach, Darwin extrapolated from observed change within species, or microevolution (think finches' beaks), to the non-observed change involving the emergence of new species from pre-existing species, or macroevolution.

Let's apply this forensic approach to modern-day biological discoveries. As a result of the pioneering work of Watson and Crick, the discoverers of DNA, we now know that individual living cells contain billions of DNA molecules that bear information critical to life. Analogies include alphabetic letters in a written text, machine code in a computer program, ancient hieroglyphics, and radio signals. In each case, the common cause explaining these effects is mind or consciousness. Quoting Henry Quastler, a pioneer in the field of information theory, "The creation of new information is habitually associated with conscious activity."[64] In fact, we know of no other cause by which one can get from chemistry to code. Material forces cannot explain discrete infusions of information at various points along the time continuum from the origin of the universe to the present day. This forensic approach makes a strong case that the ultimate cause explaining the origin of life is a transcendent mind, or a being outside the realm of space, time, matter, and energy. Borrowing a term from Dr. Stephen Meyer's latest book, we could call this ultimate cause "the God hypothesis."[65]

While most scientists today agree that microevolution is a real phenomenon, there is considerable controversy surrounding

64. Henry Quastler, *The Emergence of Biological Organization* (New Haven, CT: Yale University Press, 1964), 16.
65. Stephen C. Meyer, *The Return of the God Hypothesis: Compelling Scientific Evidence for the Existence of God* (New York: HarperOne, 2020).

macroevolution. Indeed, like the origin of life field, Darwinism is a theory in crisis. While this crisis is apparent in the peer reviewed scientific literature on evolution, it is not generally acknowledged in the classroom where Darwinism (updated to reflect post-Darwin discoveries like genetic mutation) is taught as absolute truth!

In conclusion, competing hypotheses concerning the origin of life from non-life and complex organisms from simpler ones lack the explanatory power of the God hypothesis. These alternative explanations include not only Neo-Darwinism and chemical evolution but also other worldviews such as pantheism and deism. In broad terms, none of these worldviews have any evidence-based theory that explains the appearance of design in the universe or in living creatures, nor can they explain how infusions of information came about in biology.

The God hypothesis stands on firmer ground in the twenty-first century than at any other time in history. Dawkins is wrong. The universe is not blind, pitiless, and without purpose. What we observe is precisely what we would expect based upon a theistic worldview and, more specifically, the God revealed in the Bible.

With all of this evidence, we conclude that there is no necessary conflict between science and faith in God. Rather, there is a clash of worldviews. Science is limited in its explanatory scope and power. According to the Nobel laureate Sir Peter Medawar, science cannot possibly explain the most basic questions asked by school children, such as "What is my purpose?" and "Where did everything begin?" In fact, the overwhelming evidence of design throughout the universe lends great strength to the God hypothesis. After all, when we see design, we automatically infer a designer separate from the object under consideration. Such design is apparent not only in the finely tuned physical laws governing space, time, matter, and energy, but also in the presence of information molecules in all life forms.

WAKE-UP CALL

Do you avoid discussions of the perceived conflict between faith and science because you are not a scientist or because you do not want to appear stupid? Are you afraid that science has unearthed, or may unearth in the future, facts that contradict your faith in God? Or rather, based on the discussion in this chapter, are you now of the view that you are on solid ground when discussing this issue?

Chapter 10

KNOW THAT ALL RELIGIONS CAN BE FALSE, BUT ONLY ONE CAN BE TRUE

*I am the way, the truth, and the life. No one can
come to the Father except through me.*

–JESUS (JOHN 14:6)

On one occasion, my lunch meeting with another CEO took an interesting spiritual turn. As is my habit, I asked his permission to give thanks over the meal. He said yes, and I thanked God for the food in Jesus' name. After a pleasant, largely business-oriented conversation, he noted with approval my prayer at the outset, adding that he attended his local church every Sunday. Following this comment, he opined that all religions are true in the sense that they all lead to God, echoing Mahatma Gandhi, who said, "The essence of all religions is one. Only their approaches are different."[66]

In those days, I enjoyed engaging in argument for the sake of

---

66. "The Essential Unity of All Religions," The Voice of Truth | The Selected Works of Mahatma Gandhi. Accessed March 3, 2021. https://www.mkgandhi.org/voiceoftruth/unityofallreligions.htm.

defeating the opposing point of view. Unfortunately, winning arguments doesn't necessarily translate into winning people. With a smile, I looked him in the eye and said he was 100 percent wrong. Since then, I have learned that it is much more constructive to ask questions rather than going on the offensive right away. Instead of attacking, I simply should have asked him how he had arrived at his conclusion. That approach would have certainly prolonged the conversation! While acknowledging that I could have approached the conversation in a more winsome way, his belief that all religions are equally true and all lead to God is, in fact, completely false.

WHY WOULD ANYONE THINK ALL ROADS LEAD TO GOD?

There are several reasons many believe that all religions are fundamentally the same. First, many who claim to be adherents of any particular religion are largely uninformed about other religions and are often uninformed about their own. For example, in response to surveys, many in the West tick the box "Christian" under questions pertaining to religious affiliation. In reality, they are not genuine Christians as explained in chapter 6. They have not in any heartfelt way repented for being indifferent to God and His purposes in creating them, they have not asked Jesus to forgive them for living autonomously, they have not trusted Jesus to save them from the consequences of their sin, and they have not sought Jesus' will regarding the many choices with which they are confronted. They are Christians in name only.

Second, many who view all religions as much the same are not adherents of any organized religion. They are the so-called "nones" in surveys that ask about religious affiliation. Members of this large and growing cohort tend to be ignorant of the claims of the various religions since they are indifferent to religion. Put another way, religion is irrelevant to them, particularly as to how they live their lives. Not being true adherents of any specific religion, they tend to throw all religions into the same basket. According to a Pew Research Center report published in 2015, the religious "nones" were growing as a percentage of all Americans, and at that time they comprised roughly 23 percent of the U.S. adult population. Moreover, 35 percent of millennials in the U.S. (those born between 1981 and 1996) identified as religiously unaffiliated.[67]

People in this group would deny (sometimes vehemently) that nonbelief is itself a religious conviction of sorts. However, one definition of religion from the Merriam-Webster dictionary is "a cause, principle, or system of beliefs held to with ardor and faith."[68] Applying this definition, one could make the case that atheism is just another one of many brands within the religious universe. For example, some proponents of atheism ardently express their beliefs and try to persuade others to join their ranks with an almost evangelical zeal. They even make pronouncements that sound distinctly religious. Carl Sagan has said, "The Cosmos is all that is or was or ever will be."[69] His words echo, intentionally or not, those of the apostle John: *Holy, holy, holy is the Lord God, the Almighty—the one who always was, who is, and who is still to come* (Revelation 4:8). Scientific credentials aside, Sagan's comment is philosophical, not scientific.

67. Michael Lipka, "Millennials Increasingly Are Driving Growth of 'Nones'," Pew Research Center. Pew Research Center, July 27, 2020. https://www.pewresearch.org/fact-tank/2015/05/12/millennials-increasingly-are-driving-growth-of-nones/.
68. "Religion," Merriam-Webster. Accessed March 3, 2021. https://www.merriam-webster.com/dictionary/religion.
69. Carl Sagan, *Cosmos* (New York: Ballantine Books, 2013), 1.

The third reason many people tend to lump all religions together is the desire to avoid conflict or offense. In today's politically correct environment, this desire to not criticize a specific religion is a major force governing discourse in the public square. Proponents of political correctness often espouse its tenets with a fervor that borders on the religious. Unfortunately, the practice of critical thinking and the open debate of differing views is under attack. Holding to a particular persuasion is often considered evidence of intolerance.

HAS TOLERANCE BEEN HIJACKED?

Unfortunately, the word *tolerance* has come to mean agreeing uncritically with another's beliefs. It bears little resemblance to the traditional definition of the word according to the Merriam-Webster dictionary: "sympathy or indulgence for beliefs or practices differing from or conflicting with one's own."[70] In essence, the word *tolerance* has been hijacked and has been made to mean the opposite of its original intent.

To paraphrase what my father told me growing up, "I may strongly disagree with your opinions, but I'll passionately defend your right to freely state them." Vigorous debate in the public square over all matters, including religious beliefs, leaves people better informed. As a result, they can make better choices for their own lives and for the wellbeing of the society of which they are a member. It is surely a sign of healthy societies when those of differing persuasions can discuss their differences in an open and friendly matter.

70. "Tolerance," Merriam-Webster. Accessed March 3, 2021. https://www.merriam-webster.com/dictionary/tolerance.

WHAT IS THE LAW OF NON-CONTRADICTION?

The concept of tolerance in the true sense of the word begs a very important question: How does one determine whose perspective is the correct one? Just because someone passionately believes something does not mean the belief is true. It could be completely untrue. Sincere, energetic advocacy will not make it less so.

On several occasions in recent years, I have heard someone use the expression "his truth" or "her truth." However, the word *truth* is being misused. While it is sometimes used as a way for people to express their personal feelings or to tell how an experience impacted them, it can also be used to show truth as relative. As such, what they are really calling truth is actually a belief or opinion. Are these beliefs evidence-based? Truth is not a matter of opinion but quite simply is that which aligns with reality. It is objective, not subjective, and it applies to everyone, everywhere, regardless of the culture or era in which they live or have lived.

As a corollary, contradictory propositions cannot both be true in the same sense at the same time. This is known as the Law of Non-Contradiction. It was to this law I appealed when I told my business friend that his assertion that all religions lead to God was wrong. Simply put, no one bases their lives on the assumption that two contradictory propositions can be equally true.

IS CHRISTIANITY UNIQUE?

I know men, and I tell you that Jesus Christ is no mere

man. Between Him and every other person in the world, there is no possible term of comparison.

−NAPOLEON BONAPARTE

When exploring the different religions of the world, there is a danger of lumping them all in the same category. In fact, the Christian worldview only superficially occupies the same category as other religions. The reason is that the uniqueness of Christianity rests inextricably on the uniqueness of Jesus' claims, supported by the historical facts of His life, death, and resurrection.

Napoleon (allegedly) said it best from exile on the island of Saint Helena: "Jesus Christ is no mere man."[71] During His earthly ministry, Jesus was presented in the New Testament writings as the Man-God—simultaneously fully man and fully God. Moreover, He is the only person in history who, according to the New Testament biographies, died and was raised back to life. And not just a temporary reprieve from death (for example, Lazarus, whom Jesus raised from the dead) but a life that has permanently overcome death. By contrast (and again borrowing from Napoleon), Mohammed and Buddha were "mere men." Following their deaths, they were seen no longer. Unlike Jesus, they live on only in the ideologies inspired by words they allegedly spoke (Mohammed) or wrote down (Buddha).

No other religions of the world make claims concerning their relevance to humankind that are even remotely comparable to those of the Christian worldview. Most importantly, during His earthly

71. "Quotation by Napoleon Bonaparte," LibertyQuotes. Accessed March 18, 2021. http://libertytree.ca/quotes/Napoleon.Bonaparte.Quote.21FE.

ministry, Jesus claimed that we could access God only through Him. Specifically, He said, *I am the way, the truth, and the life. No one can come to the Father except through me* (John 14:6). To say it differently, all other religions that claim that the way to God is through their beliefs and rituals are false if Jesus is who He claims to be.

Some people take great offense at this claim. What gives anyone the right to make such an audacious statement? The answer is that Jesus is not a mere man. He is the eternal God. He sets the rules. His gift of reconciliation with God is not exclusive in the most important sense. It is freely offered to anyone who trusts in His atoning work on the cross. No exceptions! Putting Christianity on the same shelf as the other religions of the world is a serious category error! In light of the enormous differences between the various religions of the world, it is clear that they cannot all lead to God. Logically, they can all be false, but they cannot all be true. Category error notwithstanding, let's consider some of these differences.

HOW WIDE IS THE GAP?

Even a brief survey of the world's major religions reveals that they sharply contradict one another in their core beliefs and doctrines. Nonetheless, some people maintain that all religions are similar in their essence but different in their more peripheral beliefs and practices. However, the opposite is true. Each is fundamentally different, while some beliefs and practices, particularly in the moral sphere, are similar.

It is not my purpose here to take a deep dive into the arena of comparative religion and to try to systematically compare the world's religions. Many scholars have addressed this topic in depth. There are numerous books and university-level courses on this subject. My goal is simply to illustrate that, at their core, the religions of the world all contradict one another. Serious adherents of any religion would be deeply offended by Gandhi's comment that "the essence of all religions is one."

By definition, atheism and agnosticism cannot be harmonized with the Christian worldview, nor can the various non-monotheistic religions of the East.[72] Taking just one example of the latter, Hinduism cannot possibly be reconciled with the worldview that claims that a relationship with God can only be established through faith in Jesus Christ. While Hindus have no serious concern when anyone adds Jesus to the Hindu pantheon of gods, deciding to follow Jesus exclusively is considered anathema.

Furthermore, the Hindu view of humankind is quite different from the Christian belief that everyone is made in the image of God and therefore is equal in the moral sense. In contrast, the Hindu caste system is based upon the belief that we are not all morally equal, nor can anyone move out of the caste into which they were born. In this view, human beings have different worth based upon their caste. For higher-caste Hindus, this status can work well in terms of opportunities to improve their lot in life. While there are examples of lower caste individuals, such as the Dalits (the so-called untouchables), prospering within the Hindu culture, the fundamental rule of inequality based on caste and its entailments remains hardwired in the religion to this day.

72. A monotheistic religion espouses the belief that there is a single, all-powerful god.

The two major monotheistic alternatives to Christianity are Judaism and Islam. Judaism and Christianity are directly connected since their adherents worship the same God described in the Hebrew Scriptures. Christians believe that Jesus is the Jewish Messiah anticipated in their prophetic writings. As the eternal Son of God, Jesus is one in essence with the God of Abraham, Isaac, and Jacob, the forefathers of the Jewish people. Christians believe that the person of Jesus Christ is the thread that is prophetically and typologically woven through the pages of the Hebrew Scriptures.

However, in accordance with the writings of the New Testament and as foreshadowed in the Hebrew Scriptures, Christians believe that the Mosaic covenant with God was made obsolete by the new covenant established by Jesus (see Hebrews 8:13). The sacrifices offered under the Mosaic covenant could never cleanse a person from sin (see Hebrews 10:1). As the perfect, sinless Son of God, Jesus completely fulfilled the requirements of the Mosaic covenant. He became the only one ever born who could save humankind from the consequences of their sin. His sacrificial death satisfied God's righteous judgment on sin once and for all. It is offered to everyone without exception and is applied to all those who believe in Him, both those who are Jewish and those who aren't.

Of course, modern Judaism is quite different from its ancient forerunner. After the temple in Jerusalem was destroyed by the Roman armies in AD 70 and the Jewish people were dispersed throughout the world, the system of temple sacrifices was made physically and spiritually obsolete. Therefore, Rabbinic Judaism as practised for centuries down to the present day is fundamentally different from its ancient precursor. Jewish religious leaders maintain that Moses received not only the written Torah (Law) but also the oral Torah at Mount Sinai. The latter, called the Talmud, is based on understandings and interpretations of the law that were later put into writing. Like the ancient Jewish people, modern adherents of Judaism believe (in varying degrees) that they primarily relate to God through keeping the oral law and its associated practices. By contrast, Christians have always believed that reconciliation with God is based solely upon grace—by receiving God's free offer of forgiveness by trusting in Jesus Christ alone.

Islam is an entirely different matter. Unlike both Judaism and Christianity, it is actually an ideology that contains a religious component. Allah of the Qur'an is not the God of the Bible. Among other things, He is unknowable and impersonal. Unlike Jesus, Mohammed was not only a religious leader, but he was also a military commander and political leader. Like Judaism, its religious component depends on good works. However, based upon those good works, Muslims can never be certain that they will go to be with Allah after they die (unless they die in an act of jihad).

While Islam honors Jesus as a great prophet, its depiction of Him cannot possibly be harmonized with the biblical accounts. According to Islam, Jesus did not die on a cross, He was not raised from the dead, and He never claimed divine status. All three claims, however, are central to the Christian worldview.

In conclusion, the Jesus depicted in the Qur'an is not the Jesus depicted in the Bible. Recognizing this objection, Muslims maintain that the Bible in use today is not an accurate copy of the original.

Given the huge amount of critical scholarly research carried out in regard to the Bible over the centuries, this position is untenable. The Islamic view of humankind is completely at odds with the Christian principle of human equality. Essentially, Islam views all who are not Muslims as being in a different and morally inferior category, and they have in mind a future world in which everyone submits to Allah of the Qur'an. Then and only then will there be world peace.

While these are only a few of the religions outside of Christianity, it is clear that the Christian worldview is in a different category from other religions. At its core, it cannot be harmonized with any other religion. The reason is that its uniqueness rests entirely on the exclusivity of Jesus' claims, supported by the historical facts of His life, death, and resurrection. Christianity has stood up to intensive scholarly criticism over many centuries. It is not a philosophy about how to live, as Buddhism is, or how to earn favor with God, as Islam teaches. Rather, Christianity makes distinctive claims about origins, identity, morality, and destiny. The Bible claims that we are created in God's image, that our purpose is to glorify Him, and that our destiny is eternity in His presence based upon faith in Jesus Christ. Christianity's claims concerning the fallen moral condition of humanity are empirically verifiable every day. This observation stands in stark contrast with any worldview that maintains that humanity is basically good and is getting better.

Based upon the Law of Non-Contradiction, all religions can logically be false, but not all can be true. By extension, if Christianity is true, then other religions are false in respect to their core doctrines.

WAKE-UP CALL

Do you avoid conversations about faith in God with those of other worldviews because you don't want to offend them? Do you believe that the gospel is intended for everyone, including those of other religious persuasions? How much do you love them?

†

PART 4:
CALLED TO ACT

HOW DO I FOLLOW JESUS IN THE MARKETPLACE?

Chapter 11

FOLLOW JESUS' EXAMPLE

Imitate God, therefore, in everything you do,
because you are his dear children. Live a life filled
with love, following the example of Christ. He
loved us and offered Himself as a sacrifice for us,
a pleasing aroma to God.

—THE APOSTLE PAUL (EPHESIANS 5:1-2)

Many excellent books have been written on the topic of leadership and how leaders should think, speak, and act. The greatest example for Christian leaders should always be Jesus. He is our role model not only for life in general but more specifically for how we conduct ourselves at work.

According to one definition, a leader is someone who has followers. While this can mean anyone from a celebrity with a large following to a senior executive of a large corporation, we will focus on leadership as it pertains to the marketplace. Effective leadership includes inspiring staff, delegating to staff, and holding staff to account for results.

These assertions beg two questions: Can leaders be followers? If so, whom or what do they follow? At first blush, a "follower-leader" would appear to be an oxymoron since these two roles appear to be mutually exclusive. This is especially the case for CEOs. While they are accountable to boards of directors, their role is to lead the organization. The reality, however, is that everyone, including CEOs, follows *something*, if not someone. For example, leaders who do not believe in Jesus follow paths dictated by their beliefs and values, as well as by decisions they have made concerning business and personal goals.

In contrast, Christian marketplace leaders follow *someone*, not something. They are "follower-leaders" who follow and are accountable to Jesus. Their professional leadership is subordinate to their identity as children of God. As Jesus' followers, they are called to place the first priority on trusting and obeying Jesus not only in their personal lives but also in their roles as leaders.

In the New Testament, Jesus invites everyone, including marketplace leaders, to become followers. On one occasion, a wealthy young leader asked Jesus what good things he needed to do to obtain eternal life. Jesus surprised him with His answer: *"If you want to be perfect, go and sell your possessions and give the money to the poor, and you will have treasure in heaven. Then come, follow me." But when the young man heard this, he went away sad, for he had many possessions* (Matthew 19:21–22).

Jesus' reply does not mean He is calling marketplace leaders to leave the marketplace and become pastors. Rather, He is simply calling everyone to accept His free invitation to follow Him in all aspects of life. From personal experience, I know that following this command will inevitably lead to uncomfortable choices from time to time. However, the joy of being in relationship with Jesus makes such discomfort worthwhile and a privilege.

As discussed in chapter 6, God is perfect in all His ways. Among other things, this truth implies that Jesus, as the eternally existent second person of the Godhead, is perfect. His example in every area of life, including leadership, should inform how the Christian marketplace leader thinks, speaks, and acts. Let's further explore Jesus' example as the role model for Christian leaders.

GREAT LEADERS ARE MISSION DRIVEN

Leaders understand the importance of being mission driven. By staying on mission, effective leaders avoid distractions that undermine the realization of goals. In this respect, no one in history has more perfectly exemplified being mission driven than Jesus.

MISSION ANNOUNCED

Physician, historian, and author of two books of the Bible, Luke records when Jesus announced His mission in the local synagogue. After reading a prophecy written hundreds of years earlier by Isaiah concerning the future arrival of a savior to set people free, Jesus said, in essence, "I am that Savior" (see Luke 4:16–21).

In an encounter with a member of the Jewish ruling council, Jesus amplified the meaning underlying the freedom He referenced in His message that day: that is, freedom from God's judgment (see John

3:1-21). Everyone stands condemned before God because of their thoughts, words, and deeds. According to Jesus, they are held captive by sin. However, those who trust in Jesus are no longer captive to, or condemned by, sin. Rather, they are set free, reconciled with God, and granted eternal life.

MISSION ANIMATED

Jesus animated His mission with deeds. Everywhere He went, He healed people of various serious diseases. He taught the principles of the kingdom of God's rule, and He confronted evil in both the rulers of that time and in His followers. Being without sin, Jesus executed His mission perfectly.

In a meeting with a non-Jewish leader subsequent to Jesus' resurrection, the apostle Peter summarized the life of Jesus as follows: *And you know that God anointed Jesus of Nazareth with the Holy Spirit and with power. Then Jesus went around doing good and healing all who were oppressed by the devil, for God was with him* (Acts 10:38).

MISSION FULFILLED

By enduring the cross and thereby bearing the punishment due every human being, Jesus perfectly fulfilled His mission. By rising from the dead, Jesus ratified His mission. As believers in Jesus, we understand that true freedom, meaning, and abundant living are found only by accepting His unconditional offer of forgiveness.

GREAT LEADERS SERVE OTHERS

It is thought that the phrase "servant leadership" was first used by Robert Greenleaf in his 1970 essay "The Servant as Leader." Since then, many businesses and other organizations have adopted servant leadership as a key organizational concept.

In reality, every leader serves someone. Sadly, many leaders act as though they themselves should be the primary beneficiaries of their service. According to Jesus, however, great leaders are not driven by self-interest. Rather, they are driven by the desire to serve others within the context of a noble cause greater than themselves. One could say that their life paradigm is servanthood. For example, the late Rich DeVos was an American billionaire businessman and owner of the Orlando Magic. According to an article in *National Review*, DeVos's biography illustrates the spirit of servanthood. In both his professional and personal life, DeVos focused on others within the context of noble causes, including many substantial philanthropic endeavors.[73]

Throughout the entire history of humankind, no one better illustrates servant leadership than Jesus Christ. In one incident recorded in the New Testament, Jesus gently rebuked two followers who asked Him to specifically promote them above His other followers. In the following passage, He encouraged servanthood as the primary leadership paradigm, using Himself as the ultimate example:

> *So Jesus called them together and said, "You know that the rulers in this world lord it over their people, and officials flaunt their authority over those under*

73. The Editors, "Richard DeVos, R.I.P.," National Review, October 5, 2018. https://www.nationalreview.com/2018/09/richard-devos-rip/.

them. But among you it will be different. Whoever
wants to be a leader among you must be your servant,
and whoever wants to be first among you must be the
slave of everyone else. For even the Son of Man [Jesus]
came not to be served but to serve others and to give
his life as a ransom for many." (Mark 10:42–45)

Jesus defines servant leadership as the intersection of the Golden Rule and the prioritizing of giving over receiving. Throughout His life, Jesus was consistently driven by a passionate focus on other people's best interests. The many times He healed those who came to Him are obvious examples. So was the time He saved a wedding banquet by miraculously replacing the wine! Always concerned for the well-being of others, He called them out on occasion for wrongful thoughts, words, or deeds. Without disrespecting them, Jesus sometimes made decisions that flew in the face of their opinions as to what actions He should take. An excellent example was His obstinate refusal to fulfill their passionate pleas that He abandon His journey to the cross. In fulfilling His destiny by dying for all of us, He perfectly and profoundly demonstrated servant leadership!

GREAT LEADERS ARE HUMBLE

Inextricably bound up in the servanthood paradigm is the character trait of humility. *Humble* has several different meanings, including "not proud or haughty" and "ranking low in a hierarchy or scale."[74] The latter meaning would seem to stand against typical organizational

74. "Humble," Merriam-Webster. Accessed March 3, 2021. https://www.merriam-webster.com/dictionary/humble.

hierarchies that accord greater status to those of higher rank. However, according to Saint Augustine (generally acknowledged as one of history's greatest thought leaders), humility is the cornerstone virtue. In Augustine's view, all other virtues are inauthentic if humility is lacking.[75]

As with servanthood, the humble leader places a very high value on other people, regardless of their position in the social or marketplace hierarchy. Humble leaders affirm the intrinsic worth of their followers, as well as their ability to contribute to the mission of the organizations they lead. Is there evidence that humble leadership is good for business? A *Forbes* magazine article titled "The Value of Humility in Leadership" by Karen Higginbottom addresses this question. Higginbottom provides several examples supporting this thesis, including the 2001 study by Jim Collins from his book *Good to Great*. She writes, "His researchers found two distinct characteristics among the leaders of these [the outperforming] companies: humility and a steely determination to do the right thing for the company, no matter how painful."[76]

Jesus Christ is the ultimate example of humble leadership. In his letter to the fledgling church at Philippi, the apostle Paul described Jesus as follows:

> *Who, being in very nature God, did not consider*
> *equality with God something to be used to his own*
> *advantage; rather, he made himself nothing by taking*

75. Joseph J. McInerney, *The Greatness of Humility: St. Augustine on Moral Excellence* (Eugene: Pickwick Publications, 2016).
76. Cheryl Williamson, "The Importance of Humility in Leadership," Forbes magazine, September 14, 2017. https://www.forbes.com/sites/forbescoachescouncil/2017/09/14/the-importance-of-humility-in-leadership/?sh=48becdf82253.

> *the very nature of a servant, being made in human*
> *likeness. And being found in appearance as a man,*
> *he humbled himself by becoming obedient to death—*
> *even death on a cross!* (Philippians 2:6–8 NIV)

The magnitude of Jesus' humility is breathtaking. According to Scripture, God the Creator loved every one of us so much that He entered the world He created to serve us (His creatures) by dying for us. There has never been and never will be a better example of stooping low!

GREAT LEADERS ARE TRUTH TELLERS

I know from personal experience that the truth can hurt. In fact, it doesn't take much mental effort to conclude that truth has consequences. Truth-telling is the cornerstone of ethical behavior. Most people would agree that honesty, which includes avoiding the use of deceit, admitting wrongdoing, and telling the truth even when it hurts, is an admirable quality in any leader.

One of the best examples is Henry Braun, the mayor of Abbotsford, Canada, at the time of this writing. Braun used to be the co-owner, president, and CEO of Abbotsford-based Pacific Northern Rail Contractors Corp. At a LeaderImpact event in 2017, he shared his story. In the early 1990s and three years after a contract closed, Braun became aware that his company had overbilled its largest customer by more than $100,000. In a meeting with the vice president of this major national company, he was asked why he would bring the matter up three years after the fact. The company was so large that, if Henry had not told them, they likely would have never discovered the mistake. Braun told the vice president that he knew the truth, and therefore, based upon his personal values, he was compelled to rectify the mistake. Because of his integrity, the customer sent them more business than they could handle over the next few years. Braun admitted that he had not always put so much importance on honesty. However, his relationship with Jesus that began at the age of thirty-eight had transformed his life so radically that he was able to tell the truth—even when it hurt!

Jesus never once avoided the truth. He defined Himself as truth (see John 14:6) and explained His purpose as testifying to the truth (see John 18:37). Scholars, even those hostile to the Christian faith, have consistently concluded over the centuries that Jesus was neither a liar nor a lunatic. In this context, Jesus' statement that He is the embodiment of truth demands attention since He claimed deity! Wherever He went during His short but remarkable public ministry, Jesus confronted everyone with the unvarnished truth. As a result, people either followed Him or shunned Him. The nation's leaders were deeply offended when Jesus put His finger on their motives. On other occasions, His words jarred His own followers when He revealed what was in their hearts, as well as when He revealed His ultimate mission. The thread uniting all His comments was love for both friends and enemies.

There are many today who would argue that we cannot know with certainty *what* is true. However, by trusting in Jesus, we can know *The One Who is truth*[77] and He will guide us into all truth! [78]

77. John 14:6
78. John 16:13

GREAT LEADERS PERSEVERE

Perseverance is "continued effort to do or achieve something despite difficulties, failure, or opposition."[79] One of the best tales of business perseverance is the birth of FedEx. Eugene Linden wrote about it in an article that was published in the April 1984 edition of *Inc.*:

> Some feel that the significance of [FedEx] is that it created a $3-billion industry where none existed before. . . . Others say the significance is in showing how one man, Frederick W. Smith, could see trends in the world, conceptualize a product that would capitalize on those trends, and motivate an untested work force to build a $1.2-billion empire. . . . Others assert that the company shows the virtues of persistence with the right product in a growing market. Finally, a broad spectrum of observers claim that the history of modern venture capital would be drastically different had the company failed. No matter how the story is told, however, it has assumed the status of myth.[80]

A few years after FedEx achieved lift-off, I was appointed CEO of a venture capital company. In those days, we often teamed up with other venture capital companies to do club deals. At a board meeting of one of the companies in which we had invested, I chatted about

79. "Perseverance," Merriam-Webster. Accessed March 3, 2021. https://www.merriam-webster.com/dictionary/perseverance.
80. Eugene Linden, "Frederick W. Smith of Federal Express: He Didn't Get There Overnight," Inc., April 1, 1984. https://www.inc.com/magazine/19840401/8479.html.

FedEx with my counterpart from Citicorp Venture Capital (CVC), a unit of my previous employer. CVC was one of the original investors in FedEx and had participated in multiple financing rounds. He noted that Fred Smith was not the only one who persevered. So, too, did the financiers who had the foresight (and the guts) to see FedEx through to launch. I suspect many would have tossed in the towel well before the company achieved commercial success.

As inspiring as the FedEx story is, Jesus' story of perseverance is immeasurably greater. For context, Jesus came into the world He created with the goal of opening the door to relationship with God through His sacrificial death on a cross. It is one thing to persevere toward some worldly objective, as meritorious as that may be, but it is quite another for Jesus to proceed unwaveringly toward His self-proclaimed objective of dying for humankind!

From the moment He launched into public ministry, Jesus faced hardship, including temptation, misunderstanding, hostile opposition, and disappointment. The religious authorities vilified Him for, in their opinion, disobeying the Mosaic law, although at the same time they acknowledged that Jesus actually performed miracles. Even His own followers misunderstood Him. They didn't get it when He plainly explained His mission. They doubted and opposed Him on occasion. Ultimately, one disciple betrayed Him to the authorities, and the rest abandoned Him. While Jesus' death led many to believe that He had failed, His resurrection on the third day vindicated His claims and opened the door to my relationship with God. I am forever grateful that He persevered for me.

GREAT LEADERS IMPART COURAGE

Courage is "the ability to do something that frightens one."[81] C. S. Lewis adds, "Courage is not simply one of the virtues, but the form of every virtue at the testing point."[82] Winston Churchill's leadership of Britain during World War II is one of many excellent examples. In an article published in *Forbes* magazine, Bill George of the Harvard Business School states, "The defining characteristic of the best [CEOs] is courage to make bold moves that transform their businesses."[83]

Courage is inevitably necessary when leading organizations, particularly when undertaking transformative change. The greatest leaders are not only personally courageous, but they are also able to impart courage to those they lead. The impartation of courage requires clear delegation of authority that is supported by confidence in the ability of the subordinate to exercise that authority wisely.

Reflecting on my own career, I can clearly see this phenomenon at work. For example, when I was a young analyst in an investment department, my boss demonstrated courage by risking his and the company's reputation on me. Shortly after hiring me, he delegated to me the authority (within prescribed limits) to solely represent the company in many meetings with CFOs and CEOs who were usually several years my senior. Over the years, my various bosses have encouraged me with words of confidence in my ability to achieve the organization's goals in a manner that gave credit to them.

81. "Courage," Lexico Dictionaries. Accessed March 3, 2021. https://www.lexico.com/en/definition/courage.
82. C.S. Lewis, *The Screwtape Letters* (London: Geoffrey Bles, 1942), ch. 29.
83. Bill George, "Courage: The Defining Characteristic of Great Leaders," Forbes magazine, April 24, 2017. https://www.forbes.com/sites/hbsworkingknowledge/2017/04/24/courage-the-defining-characteristic-of-great-leaders/?sh=43862f8d11ca.

No one better exemplifies the ability to impart courage than Jesus. He delegated full authority to His followers to represent Him in the world. Following His resurrection after claiming absolute authority, Jesus commissioned His followers to represent Him in the world by making new followers. On a previous occasion, He encouraged them to believe they would do even greater works than He had accomplished during His earthly ministry (see John 14:12). How is that for risk-taking? Unlike the aforementioned new employer who didn't know me, Jesus knows everything about you and me, including our every thought! I don't know about you, but a quick review of my own conduct confirms that I am not always a credit to Jesus' reputation. The wonderful news is that He has not left us as orphans but instead has sent His Holy Spirit to indwell and empower those who believe in Him (see John 14:15–18).

His impartation of courage proved out then, and it continues to do so today. Many of His followers died for their refusal to deny Him. Sadly, this remains the case today as believers around the world are being persecuted, sometimes killed, for their refusal to deny Jesus.

GREAT LEADERS VALUE WISDOM

The *Oxford English Dictionary* defines *wisdom* as the "capacity of judging rightly in matters relating to life and conduct; soundness of judgement in the choice of means and ends."[84] On many occasions, I witnessed firsthand great wisdom brought to bear on problems and opportunities by boards of directors on which I have served. Board

84. "Wisdom," Lexico Dictionaries. Accessed March 3, 2021. https://www.lexico.com/en/definition/wisdom.

members bring a wide range of experience and intelligence to decision-making on various issues. And most of these decisions incorporate the application of moral choices.

As God incarnate, Jesus is by far the wisest person in history. Not even King Solomon of the Hebrew Scriptures comes close! In his letter to the newly established church in Rome, the apostle Paul made the following assertion: *Oh, how great are God's riches and wisdom and knowledge! How impossible it is for us to understand his decisions and his ways! For who can know the Lord's thoughts? Who knows enough to give him advice?* (Romans 11:33–34).

Over the centuries, many people have commented on the wisdom of Jesus' words and actions during His earthly ministry. Jesus ascribed great wisdom to the little children who readily received the truth that He was the One ushering in the kingdom of God's rule. He considered children wiser than their parents in certain areas. I read somewhere the following advice from children. These gems support the argument that simple thoughts are often the wisest:

- *If you want a kitten, start out by asking for a horse.* —Naomi, age fifteen
- *Never try to baptize a cat.* —Eileen, age eight
- *Never trust a dog to watch your food.* —Patrick, age ten

GREAT LEADERS ATTRIBUTE THEIR SUCCESS TO OTHERS

Following two years in the custody of Turkish authorities while awaiting trial on fabricated charges of aiding terrorism, Pastor Andrew Brunson was convicted on October 12, 2018, and sentenced to time served. Within twenty-four hours, he went from facing the prospect of a thirty-five-year prison sentence to praying for President Trump in the Oval Office! How is that for a swift 180-degree change in circumstances?

Andrew Brunson is an extraordinary leader. By founding a local church in Izmir more than twenty years ago, he and his wife, Norine, became spiritual entrepreneurs. Entrepreneurship is inherently risky, and they were well aware of the dangers. Death threats were common as they led their small congregation and openly shared their faith in Jesus with everyone, including Turks, Kurds, and Syrian refugees. The certainty that God had called them to Turkey, along with their love for the Turkish people, sustained them through many challenges.

Upon learning of his release, Mary and I rejoiced. Like thousands of believers around the world, we had prayed for Brunson for two years. We felt a special bond with him since at that time he was the Middle East coordinator for Partners in Harvest, an affiliation created by our local church in Toronto. Brunson attributed his successful release to others, which included the thousands praying for him around the world and the many people, politicians, and organizations who spoke up for him. Most importantly, Brunson and his wife gave thanks to God for acting through so many others to secure their release.

On a much larger scale, Jesus experienced great success during His earthly ministry. Many people were healed, the dead were raised, and even His enemies acknowledged His extraordinary wisdom. Yet Jesus attributed His success to someone else. In response to hostile questioning on one occasion, He replied, *My Father is always working, and so am I. . . . I tell you the truth, the Son can do nothing by Himself.*

He does only what He sees the Father doing (John 5:17, 19). Jesus, who is God the eternal Son, took on human flesh, thereby constraining His power during His earthly sojourn. As a result, He acknowledged complete reliance on God the Father for His every success. In this interaction with His critics, Jesus gave credit where credit was due.

In consideration of Jesus' example, I recognize that I sometimes forget to give credit to others. While this is hard for leaders to admit, we depend to a significant degree on others for any success we achieve. In particular, as a follower of Jesus, I need to constantly keep my dependence upon God in the front of my mind.

GREAT LEADERS PROTECT OTHERS

Based on my ongoing experience with Jesus, I realize that He is the perfect leader. The examples mentioned above have merely scratched the surface of who He is. Several years ago, we were to join several others from our church on a short-term mission trip to India. Our purpose was to teach pastors and other Indian leaders through our International Leaders School of Ministry (ILSOM), a training program developed by our church and one that is much in demand worldwide. We had previously participated in an ILSOM near Mumbai, and on this occasion we were slated to go to New Delhi. Our teams were to meet in Mumbai prior to fanning out across India.

After tentatively agreeing to go, we were invited by a close niece to her wedding in England. The date conflicted with the last part of the ILSOM. After considering the conflict, we decided to arrive in Mumbai early and depart the school early to attend her wedding. On the day we were to commit on travel arrangements, we prayed about the trip. I was quite certain God wanted us in India, but Mary thought it was still important to pray about it. Surprisingly, she had a strong sense from God that we weren't to go, and shortly thereafter, so did I. Since we were looking forward to returning to India, we were confused. However, we canceled since we were certain that, for some reason, God didn't want us to go. Soon afterward, our niece informed us that her wedding had been moved up. The new date would have prevented us from attending the first half of the ILSOM. Confident that God didn't want us in India on this occasion, I agreed to travel to Ghana on business during the same dates as the ILSOM.

On the evening of November 26, 2008, my colleague joined me at dinner in Kumasi, Ghana, with the news of several terrorist attacks in Mumbai. Among the targets was the Taj Mahal Palace Hotel. Mary and I had visited this hotel on our previous visit and planned to stay there during the two days leading up to the ILSOM. As a result, we would have been staying there at exactly the time the attack occurred if it had not been for God's intervention. During the attack on the Taj, many hotel guests were held hostage, many were injured, and thirty-one died. Mary and I thank God that He is constantly protecting us, and we continue to be diligent to pray before traveling.

As leaders, we are called to protect others. One of the main ways we do so is by taking responsibility for failures rather than blaming others. Even if the mistake was made by a member of our team, we must keep in mind that it is our team, we lead it, and the buck stops with us!

WAKE-UP CALL

Are you taking the time to know Jesus intimately through reading the Bible, prayer, and meeting with other believers? Are you Christlike at work? After all, Jesus is the perfect leader, and according to Scripture, we are called to imitate Him. When you do something wrong, do you seek forgiveness from those who were wronged?

Chapter 12

BE OPEN ABOUT YOUR FAITH IN THE MARKETPLACE

Through thick and thin, keep your hearts at attention, in adoration before Christ, your Master. Be ready to speak up and tell anyone who asks why you're living the way you are, and always with the utmost courtesy. Keep a clear conscience before God so that when people throw mud at you, none of it will stick. They'll end up realizing that they're the ones who need a bath.

—THE APOSTLE PETER (1 PETER 3:15-16 MSG)

Transparency in the workplace regarding faith in God is sometimes greeted with skepticism, if not outright hostility. Of course, the frequent outcry these days against any speech that doesn't conform to prevailing secular orthodoxy can be reason enough for some believers to simply switch off their light! We must be mindful, however, that

Jesus made it clear we should expect opposition. Many of our fellow believers around the world are not just suffering rejection when they make Jesus known but are dying for their belief in Jesus. The example of individuals I have met who were subsequently martyred stiffens my resolve!

In this chapter, I will share some strategies I have employed to maximize the intensity and consistency of my light in my professional life. These are not treatises on best practices, and you undoubtedly might have different strategies that work for you. The critical point is that we leaders should be open about our faith when in the marketplace, regardless of the cost.

PUT FIRST THINGS FIRST

For Mary and me, putting first things first every day is absolutely critical. In John's Gospel, Jesus says, *Remain in me, as I also remain in you. No branch can bear fruit by itself; it must remain in the vine. Neither can you bear fruit unless you remain in me* (John 15:4 NIV). We take Jesus' admonition seriously that without Him we can accomplish nothing. As a result, we dedicate time each morning, seven days a week, to focus on God's presence. Mary and I get up between 5:00 and 6:00 a.m. (we sometimes sleep in until 6:30 a.m. on weekends), and once the first cup of coffee is poured, we usually spend a few minutes reminding each other of our many blessings. We see this practice as a great way to bring our light out of sleep mode. This is a great blessing to do with a spouse, but the same practice works if you are single. Instead of three in the room, there are two!

Without being formulaic, Mary and I usually thank God for His forgiveness and intimate involvement in every facet of our lives—from the gift of life itself to ongoing provision, hope, family, friends, health, finances, and anything else that comes to our hearts or minds. Repetition is a good thing because it helps us keep our minds and focus on Christ. I cannot count the thousands of times we have reminded each other about the greatness of our salvation and the various facets of our identity.

After beginning with thanksgiving, we usually move into worship through music, which has always played a big role in our lives. Next, we engage in a variety of daily disciplines, such as reading passages of the Bible to each other, reading devotional material, and praying over various people and issues as God leads.

Early morning preparation aside, marketplace turbulence can rapidly throw me off my game if I am not careful. As all marketplace leaders know, a business day can unexpectedly turn intense. Confession: there have been occasions over the years when such turbulence has distracted from my desire to be my authentic self at work and represent Jesus well. With that said, here are some practices I follow to maximize the effectiveness of my Christian witness in the marketplace.

MAKE KNOWN THAT YOU ARE A FOLLOWER OF JESUS

It is imperative that the people with whom we interact in the marketplace know the motive that underlies our conduct. Even if we have been "deep undercover" for some time, we must muster the courage to be transparent about our faith as soon as possible, regardless of our discomfort. As we discussed earlier in this book, Jesus called us to do so, and we demonstrate the love of God and love for others through obedience to His commands.

Throughout my many years in business leadership, I have dealt with a lot of individuals who behave admirably. They treat others well and conduct themselves in a highly ethical manner. However, I don't know why they behave the way they do unless they tell me. By contrast, we are called to make Jesus known, and we can only do this if others understand that our reason for behaving as we do is Jesus! Otherwise, they will not be able to connect our conduct with the central reality of our lives. A lack of transparency regarding our true identity undercuts our primary calling to glorify God everywhere, including in the marketplace.

There is no formula for how best to make known that we are followers of Jesus. In my case, I intentionally look for opportunities. Typically, these occur when another person opens the door. For example, I recall discussing a senior executive position with someone who knew me well prior to my encounter with Jesus. Since they were interested in my thoughts regarding the new opportunity, I told them I was no longer the same person they knew when we worked together previously. Rather, my life had changed dramatically after I became a follower of Jesus. My conduct in the marketplace was now based upon my desire to please Him.

I have found that others consistently find favor with my transparency concerning my faith in God. My faith in Jesus also causes me to draw a line in the sand concerning decision-making. I have had to do this when someone proposes a course of action that goes against Jesus' commands. I use the specific situation to share why my faith and worldview do not allow me to acquiesce to the proposal. That revelation is not always greeted happily, but it is almost always met with respect.

Finally, when someone in the workplace experiences a real-life challenge, such as a financial loss, a sickness, or a death in the family, I often treat it as a door opener. Typically, I will ask their permission to pray for them. In my experience, they invariably agree. I then take the opportunity to tell them that, as a follower of Jesus, I have seen many instances of answered prayer. I have seen many such prayer requests by those in the marketplace answered quickly. This sets the stage for initiating deeper conversations in the future. For example, on September 11, 2001, my human-resources manager told me her sister was in one of the World Trade Center towers. After asking her permission, I prayed with her for her sister's safety; thankfully, her sister survived.

Importantly, I avoid describing myself as a Christian as much as possible since this label comes with a lot of baggage these days. While some have an unfavorable opinion of Christians because some Christians criticize those outside the faith, many are dubious of Christians because of the actions of individuals within Christian communities. Therefore, I usually identify myself as a follower of Jesus and explain that I look to Him for guidance. This self-descriptor has the added advantage of communicating that I follow a person, not a set of precepts. Unique to the Christian worldview, this one fact has led to some interesting conversations. After all, how can I follow someone who has been dead for two thousand years?

BE KNOWN FOR A SPIRIT OF EXCELLENCE

Having disclosed that I am a follower of Jesus, I am officially on record. I have put my ambassadorial credentials on the table. Others will now take a heightened interest in my conduct. I am now accountable not only to Jesus but also to them. Since I have made known why I do what I do, others will make judgments about Jesus because of what I say and do. While this realization might be intimidating, it is also encouraging in the sense that I can point other marketplace leaders to Jesus through my conduct. If we behave with excellence, our conduct lends credibility when we explicitly share the gospel.

God is perfect in all His ways, and Jesus is the epitome of excellence. A very important way by which we can reveal Jesus to our peers in the marketplace is by being known for excellence. In his letter to the church in Colossae, the apostle Paul says, *Don't just do the minimum [for your employer] that will get you by. Do your best. Work from the heart for your real Master, for God* (Colossians 3:22–23 MSG). In essence, Paul is encouraging followers of Jesus to conduct themselves with excellence in the workplace, thereby bolstering their credibility when sharing their faith with others.

I always try to conduct myself in a first-class manner in everything I do in the marketplace. This includes tasks I perform or delegate, meetings I attend, letters I write, and even spelling and grammar in short emails. It also means establishing a reputation for trustworthiness. I do my utmost to show up at meetings before the scheduled time. If I commit to being anywhere or doing anything by a specific time, I either deliver or I give timely notice that I cannot complete it on time or cannot be there on time because of unforeseen circumstances. I then work out a new, mutually satisfactory timeline.

Most leaders who are not yet believers would agree that these various behaviors are praiseworthy. Conducting ourselves in accordance with Jesus' example enhances our reputations as people of excellence and opens the door for sharing the gospel. Dietrich Bonhoeffer, who courageously honored God with his life and was ultimately executed for his stand in Nazi Germany, is alleged to have said, "Your life as a Christian should make non-believers question their disbelief in God."[85] Exactly!

Of course, there is a difference between trying to perform with excellence and actually doing it. The good news is that being known for excellence does not mean being perfect. Besides Jesus, no one is perfect. When we do inevitably fail, admitting our mistakes and taking responsibility for them are other aspects of a spirit of excellence.

BE KNOWN FOR GENEROSITY

As a follower of Jesus, I am called to a lifestyle of generosity. Generosity flows naturally from the realization that we are stewards, not owners. According to the book of Hebrews, we are admonished as follows: *Do not forget to do good and to share with others, for with such sacrifices God is pleased* (Hebrews 13:16 NIV). According to the apostle Peter, *Each of you should use whatever gift you have received to serve others, as faithful stewards of God's grace in its various forms* (1 Peter 4:10 NIV). Finally, the apostle Paul said:

85. "A Quote by Dietrich Bonhoeffer., Goodreads. Accessed March 18, 2021. https://www.goodreads.com/quotes/978699-your-life-as-a-christian-should-make-non-believers-question.

Command those who are rich in this present world
not to be arrogant nor to put their hope in wealth,
which is so uncertain, but to put their hope in God,
who richly provides us with everything for our
enjoyment. Command them to do good, to be rich
in good deeds, and to be generous and willing to
share. In this way they will lay up treasure for them-
selves as a firm foundation for the coming age, so
that they may take hold of the life that is truly life.
(1 Timothy 6:17–19 NIV)

I have learned that one of the best ways to draw attention to Jesus in the marketplace is by making known some of the Christian ministries in which we invest our LIFE (Labor [time], Influence, Finances, and Expertise). In this way, we potentially open doors to deeper conversations since these causes connect others in a very tangible way to the reality of our faith in God. The purpose is not to draw attention to ourselves but to Him.

On one occasion, I invited some staff in my company to help an organization rescue homeless children on the streets of southern Brazil. I emphasized they were under no pressure to give. I presented it as an opportunity to make a big impact on the lives of those who were much less fortunate than they were. Many loved the idea and pitched in with gifts and money. I have found that most people find favor with high-impact charitable initiatives. During our trips to Brazil, we told the children that many people in Canada cared about them. This seemed to provide the children with as much encouragement as the rescue itself! Most importantly, this project showed Jesus in a favorable light and created more opportunities over time to share my faith in the workplace.

BE QUICK TO FORGIVE AND SEEK FORGIVENESS

The centerpiece of the Christian worldview is the notion of forgiveness. Jesus' mission was to provide the means whereby we can be forgiven and reconciled to God. Just as God forgives us, we are commanded to forgive others (see Matthew 6:12, 14–15).

Situations inevitably arise in business in which one party wrongs another. However, seeking reconciliation through forgiveness is not just an option for followers of Jesus, but it is an imperative. Most readers will understand that carrying unforgiveness in any situation usually harms the person wronged more than the wrongdoer.

On the other hand, many leaders do not appreciate the impact on others, especially the people we deal with in the marketplace, when we seek their forgiveness for something we have done. Sometimes our egos can get in the way of acknowledging mistakes we have made. I know this to be true because on occasion I have succumbed to this temptation. When I examined the situation dispassionately, however, I realized I was in the wrong, and I sought the other person's forgiveness. This action is so countercultural that it sometimes surprises the person receiving my regrets. Most importantly, it puts Jesus in a favorable light!

PROACTIVELY SEEK OPPORTUNITIES TO SHARE THE GOSPEL

I interpret the apostle Paul's admonition to be excellent workers to mean that explicitly sharing the gospel in the workplace is generally inappropriate during work hours unless it is done in response to a question or in a life-and-death situation.

With that said, followers of Jesus are always to be opportunistic. For example, Paul says later in his letter to the Colossians, *Live wisely among those who are not believers, and make the most of every opportunity. Let your conversation be gracious and attractive so that you will have the right response for everyone* (Colossians 4:5–6). This directive implies that we should always listen carefully when others speak, not only because it honors them and facilitates good communication, but also because a door of spiritual opportunity is sometimes opened. I have often shared my spiritual journey with other leaders in these situations.

This proves to be a much more effective way of sparking deeper conversations than simply stating what we, as followers of Jesus, believe. It has the advantage of personalizing my relationship with Jesus. While people might have objections to numerous aspects of the Christian worldview, they cannot argue with our experience of Jesus. This reality brings to mind the revelation received by the apostle John that we overcome by the blood of the Lamb and the word of our testimony (see Revelation 12:11). As previously mentioned, I follow the practice of asking others for permission to speak about spiritual matters. This not only includes praying about a particular issue but also encouraging them based on my Christian worldview.

JOIN A LEADERIMPACT GROUP

For years, I have enjoyed being part of a LeaderImpact group. It is a safe place where I can share my personal, professional, and spiritual challenges. These groups include not only followers of Jesus but also those who want to explore the relevance of faith in God in their professional and personal lives. The groups can help believers share their faith with their peers. These groups are active in many cities all over the world, and I encourage you to join a group if there is one near you.

WAKE-UP CALL

Do the people with whom you work know that you are a follower of Jesus? Through your conduct, have you earned the right to share your faith? When was the last time you shared the gospel with a peer?

Conclusion
CALLED TO LIFE

This book began with a challenge to marketplace leaders. In your professional life, are you experiencing the *rich and satisfying life* promised by Jesus (John 10:10)? If not, why not?

It is the premise of this book that business leaders cannot truly experience this abundant life unless they are passionately committed to knowing and following Jesus wherever He leads them in the workplace. In particular, we must treat our role as marketplace leaders as a calling rather than simply as a means to an end, such as funding good works. Of course, every believer is called to be generous, but this practice does not, by itself, constitute a calling.

The reason that many people do not see business as a legitimate calling is quite straightforward. Pastors and others who are engaged in vocational ministry do not promote this concept. I recently listened to a sermon in which the pastor encouraged his listeners to see their occupations through the lens of a calling. So far so good! He then went on to provide several examples of callings, including teaching, medicine, dentistry, law, engineering, the arts, and government. Never once did he mention business as an option. Since the majority of individuals in most cultures are engaged in some facet of business, ranging from ownership to leadership to various roles as employees, it is a major omission.

Another reason for ambivalence about business is lack of appreciation for the fundamental importance of this domain in regard to human flourishing. In fact, business is the primary vehicle driving innovation and providing jobs. Ultimately, it funds everything else. Because of the economic importance of the business realm, marketplace leaders have substantial influence (for better or for worse) in every culture. Finally, the not-uncommon belief that business is somehow morally tainted influences Christian perceptions of business as a legitimate calling. In response, I argue in this book that business is not intrinsically contaminated by its various notable characteristics such as profit-seeking, but, as in any other field, individual business leaders can behave in ways that do not honor God.

Assuming the reader concludes he or she is called to business, we need a big "why" to motivate us to fully realize God's plans and purposes for us in this calling. Since the marketplace is a spiritual battlefield, it is easy to default to essentially leaving God at home. Even if we are careful to conduct our business affairs in a way that honors God, we should ask if we are operating under the guise of secret service agents.

The number one reason we are called to business leadership is to love those we serve. Loving our neighbors in the marketplace is multifaceted, but the central way in which we demonstrate love to those with whom we interact at work is by sharing the good news of Jesus with them. After all, most of our professional peers are unlikely of their own volition to darken the door of a church. As their equals, we are best positioned to share the gospel with them because of our credibility and the fact that we have found faith in God to be highly relevant in our own lives.

We need to be clear about what we believe since the power to persuade others flows from strong convictions anchored in knowledge. Knowing Jesus is the most important information we possess! This only results when we have an active and vibrant relationship with Him. If we cannot point to such a relationship, we need to decide whether we want to surrender our lives to Him, and if so, we need to take action (see appendix B).

Assuming we have decided to follow Him, we need to be convinced of our stand in various areas in which attacks on our faith are most prominent. As discussed in part 3, we have every good reason to believe that the Bible is trustworthy, that the resurrection is a historical fact, that science and faith in God are compatible, and that Christianity is not just one truth among many since it is fundamentally different from and in opposition to all other worldviews.

At the end of the day, we are called to act. After all, faith without works is dead (see James 2:26). Armed with truth, we must let Jesus' rich and satisfying life shine through us as we provide marketplace leadership. So here is a challenge for each of us: If we were put on trial for being a follower of Jesus in the marketplace, would there be enough evidence to convict us?

Appendix A
MESSIANIC PROPHECIES

Before considering numerous prophecies that point toward a future Messiah, consider this important fact: scholars from across the worldview spectrum overwhelmingly agree that these utterances were recorded hundreds of years before the life, death, and resurrection of Jesus Christ.

Recognizing the uncanny linkage between these prophecies and Jesus' life, death, and resurrection, some skeptics assert that this connection is some sort of Christian conspiracy to validate claims about Jesus. Given the enormous time gap, however, this is a weak argument. To be charitable, perhaps they have not considered the evidence!

As we review this material, let's not lose sight of the profound significance of this huge time gap. As stated earlier, we have difficulty forecasting most events even over the next year. Generally speaking, anyone who maintains that he or she knows what will happen ten years from now, let alone hundreds of years in the future, would likely be considered a crackpot!

For centuries, Jewish scholars considered these prophetic Scripture passages to be messianic. This is not a case of Christians looking backward and reading messianic interpretations into these Scriptures. Jewish religious leaders and scholars of the day and down through the centuries also interpreted them as messianic. In fact, there are many more messianic prophecies in the Hebrew Scriptures that were fulfilled in Jesus Christ than are included here.

In addition to the many direct prophecies concerning the Messiah, there are also many stories in Israel's history that parallel the messianic narrative. These include Abraham obeying God's command to offer up his son as a sacrifice and Moses obeying God's command to lead the Israelites out of bondage to their Egyptian slave masters. In parallel to the former, Jesus, the Son of God, was offered as a sacrifice for the sin of humankind. In parallel to the latter, Jesus delivered humankind from the bondage to sin through His substitutionary atonement on the cross. The direct prophecies, together with the parallel historical accounts, support the assertion that the metanarrative of the entire Bible is Jesus Christ.

Many of these prophecies would have made little or no sense to the prophets uttering them or to their contemporaries hearing them. They would have seemed obscure at the time they were delivered. Only in the life, death, and resurrection of Jesus do they make sense. This observation supports once again the contention that the New Testament is concealed in the Old Testament, which in turn is revealed in the New Testament. We could characterize the various messianic prophecies as a jigsaw puzzle inspired by God that make sense only when we stand back from viewing individual pieces of the puzzle and take in the whole work. These prophecies were fulfilled exclusively in Jesus Christ.

The fulfillment of these prophecies supports the thesis that the writing of the Bible, unlike any other book in history, was supernaturally inspired by God. The following is a small portion of the prophecies concerning the future Messiah.

THE ROLE AND MISSION OF THE MESSIAH

From the many Old Testament prophecies concerning the role of the coming Messiah, a multifaceted portrait emerges. The three principal aspects are king, priest, and suffering servant. The ordinary understanding of these three human types is difficult to reconcile with the concept of one person fulfilling all three roles.

For example, in the Old Testament, the priests of ancient Israel came exclusively from the tribe of Levi and performed an intermediary role between God and the people of Israel. In contrast, the kings did not come from the tribe of Levi and they ruled over the people of Israel. Perhaps most surprisingly, the Messiah was prophetically portrayed as a suffering servant. This picture would likely have seemed strange, if not confusing, to the people of Israel in the pre-Christian era since a kingly persona would have seemed at odds with that of a suffering servant. In those days, suffering was generally viewed as a sign that the sufferer was cursed by God, whereas the kings of Israel were deemed blessed by God.

Regarding the mission of the Messiah, He was seen in the Old Testament as a deliverer not only of the people of Israel but of all humankind. During Jesus' earthly ministry, however, the people of Israel eagerly anticipated the arrival of a human king (like King David) who would rescue their nation exclusively rather than the entire world. More specifically, they saw him as someone who would defeat the Roman military rulers and deliver them from bondage to the emperor in Rome.

According to the prophet Isaiah, however, the Messiah was *pierced for our transgressions, he was crushed for our iniquities; the punishment*

*that brought us peace was on him, and by his wounds we are healed. We
all like sheep have gone astray, each of us has turned to our own way; and
the Lord has laid on him the iniquity of us all* (Isaiah 53:5–6). According
to this prophecy, the mission of the Messiah was to rescue humankind,
but not in the ordinary sense of liberation from human oppression.
Rather, He would save us from the consequence of our sin by paying
the just penalty for human iniquity.

In this way, He would open the door to reconciliation between
humankind and God. By undergoing substitutionary suffering resulting in death, the Messiah would be the ultimate fulfillment of the
priestly, or intermediary, role. He would also fulfill the kingly role
by surviving death and assuming rulership over the kingdom of God,
which comprises everyone (both Jews and non-Jews) who trusts
in Him.

THE MESSIAH'S ANCESTRAL LINEAGE

The ancestry of the prophesied Messiah unfolds gradually over the
course of the Old Testament writings. It begins in the opening chapters of the Bible with God's pronouncement that the Messiah would
be the male offspring of a woman. That narrows it down to about 50
percent of the human race!

However, the prophesied lineage then progressively narrows over
the following centuries to the lines of the Jewish patriarchs: Abraham,
his son Isaac, and Isaac's son Jacob (aka Israel). The lineage then continues to narrow down to Judah, one of the twelve tribes of Israel, and
ultimately to the line of King David.

The idea that the Messiah would be from the line of King David became deeply entrenched in Jewish thinking. Right up to Jesus' day, one of the Messiah's most familiar titles was "Son of David," a title adopted by Jesus and ascribed to Him by the crowds that followed Him (e.g., Matthew 1:1; Matthew 12:23; Mark 10:48).

THE TIMING OF THE MESSIAH'S ARRIVAL

The patriarch Jacob established that the Messiah would arrive before the tribe of Judah lost its self-governing status, which occurred in AD 70 when the Roman army utterly destroyed Jerusalem, including the Second Temple.

The prophet Daniel, who lived in Babylon during the time of the Jewish exile, narrowed the timing of the deliverer's arrival with startling precision. Daniel recorded a vision he received from the archangel Gabriel concerning the timing of the Messiah's future arrival (see Daniel 9:24–27). Although the account sounds strange to contemporary ears, many scholars have carefully studied the text in the original language and concluded that it establishes the arrival of the Messiah within an extremely narrow window of time. Specifically, the Messiah was to suffer and die between the years AD 30 and 37 according to the Christian method of numbering years. While there is debate over the precise year that Jesus died, most scholars agree that this event fell within these two bookends—prophesied about five centuries earlier!

THE PLACE OF THE MESSIAH'S ARRIVAL AND MINISTRY

The prophet Micah, who delivered his message in the eighth century BC, prophesied that the Messiah would be born in Bethlehem

Ephrathah, a small village south of Jerusalem (see Micah 5:2). Interestingly, the prophet says that the Messiah would be pre-existent yet would be born in Bethlehem Ephrathah. This assertion aligns perfectly with the Christian belief that Jesus, the Messiah, was truly God (eternally existent) and truly human (time-limited). According to Luke's biography of Jesus, He was born in the unimportant village of Bethlehem, as prophesied by Micah, and there exists no alternative claims concerning the place of His birth.

The prophet Isaiah pronounced that the Messiah *will honor Galilee of the nations, by the Way of the Sea, beyond the Jordan* (Isaiah 9:1 NIV). We understand from the New Testament that not only was Jesus born in Bethlehem Ephrathah, but He lived and ministered primarily (though not exclusively) in the region of Galilee.

Isaiah also wrote that the Messiah would be born in a miraculous manner from a virgin and would be called Immanuel (meaning "God with us"), therefore confirming the godly nature of the Messiah as pronounced by Micah, a contemporary of Isaiah (see Isaiah 7:14).

THE EARTHLY MINISTRY AND ACCOMPLISHMENTS OF THE MESSIAH

The various prophecies make it clear that the Messiah would be an extraordinary person. Not only would He have a kingly nature, but He would also have the ability to perform miracles. For example, Isaiah describes some miraculous workings of the Messiah: *Then will the eyes of the blind be opened and the ears of the deaf unstopped. Then will the lame leap like a deer and the mute tongue shout for joy* (Isaiah 35:5–6 NIV). The Gospel accounts of Jesus' life provide many examples of Him healing the blind, the deaf, the lame, and the mute.

In addition to prophesying that the Messiah would perform miracles, Isaiah foretold that the Messiah would preach the good news to the poor. As it happens, Jesus announced His mission early on when He opened the scroll in the synagogue at Nazareth to these specific words of Isaiah and announced, *Today this scripture is fulfilled in your hearing* (Luke 4:21 NIV).

THE JEWISH REACTION TO THE MESSIAH

Isaiah prophesied that the Jews would for the most part reject their Messiah, writing that they would be *ever hearing, but never understanding; be ever seeing, but never perceiving [and] the heart of this people [would be] calloused* (Isaiah 6:9–10 NIV).

While many Jews followed Jesus during His earthly ministry, many rejected Him (including even His own family prior to His resurrection). The leaders of the Jews ultimately rejected Him after they accused Him of committing blasphemy when He claimed to be equal with God, sentencing Him to death. The prophetic words of Psalm 118:22 were fulfilled: *The stone that the builders rejected has now become the cornerstone.*

THE SUFFERING AND RESURRECTION OF THE MESSIAH

In Psalm 22, King David spoke prophetically about a future time when an individual would greatly suffer at the hands of persecutors. With the benefit of hindsight, Jesus' suffering, death, and resurrection fit this psalm precisely. According to the biographies written by Matthew and Mark, Jesus quoted from its opening verse when

He hung on the cross: *My God, my God, why have you abandoned me?* (Matthew 27:46; Mark 15:34). There in His death throes, Jesus applied it directly to Himself.

Amazingly, centuries before crucifixion was invented, Psalm 22 predicted much of what Jesus experienced while He was being cru-cified! It includes disdainful treatment from those afflicting Him, mockery, insults, and challenges for the Lord to deliver Him. It also includes the division of His clothing among His persecutors. All these specific predictions accord with the New Testament accounts.

In graphic terms, the prophecy describes the agony that Jesus endured, which, again, is in close agreement with the New Testament writings. From Psalm 22, we learn that all His bones were out of joint, that His tongue stuck to the roof of His mouth, that all His bones were on display, that they pierced His hands and feet, and that He was laid in the dust of death. Yet we also learn that the Lord *has not despised or scorned the suffering of the afflicted one; he has not hidden His face from him but has listened to his cry for help* (Psalm 22:24 NIV). In another Psalm, David declares that the Lord *will not abandon me to the realm of the dead, nor will you let your faithful one see decay* (Psalm 16:10 NIV). These verses harmonize well with the historical account of Jesus' bodily resurrection.

As previously discussed, perhaps the most uncanny prophecy concerning the suffering servant is found in chapters 52 and 53 of the book of Isaiah. Throughout the centuries up to the present day, many Jews have come to believe in Jesus because of these prophecies. When they read them in the context of Jesus' suffering, death, and resurrection, they conclude that Jesus' suffering and crucifixion were clearly foretold in their own Scriptures!

It even goes beyond the Jewish people. Today, approximately two billion people all over the world from every nation, people group, and ethnicity claim to follow Jesus Christ! Such enormous impact can be attributed to no other individual in history.

HOW DO I BECOME A FOLLOWER OF JESUS?

Jesus said that in order to enter the kingdom of heaven, a person must be *born again* (John 3:3). This consists of an act of the heart in believing in Jesus Christ as Lord and Savior. When we were born into the world physically, we were born spiritually dead, and therefore we need a spiritual birth. The spiritual birth involves two facets.

The first is to realize we cannot make it on our own. We are sinners separated from God and have chosen to go our own way. We cannot get back to God on our own because of sin.

Sin can simply be characterized as our own self-centered pride and selfishness. More specifically, sin is the violation of a holy God's standard of righteousness. Therefore, we must own up to the fact that we need a Savior, someone who can and will accomplish all that God requires. The only person ever to do this was Jesus Christ. He lived the only life that was ever acceptable to God.

Jesus died as a substitute on the cross for our sins because we have no chance of pleasing God on our own merit. The initial step, then, is to realize that we all have sinned, have broken God's law, and deserve judgment as a result. The Bible says that *the wages of sin is death* (Romans 6:23 KJV).

Once a person sees his hopeless condition and realizes that Jesus Christ offers an answer, the next step is to receive that offer personally, for *the gift of God is eternal life through Jesus Christ our Lord* (Romans 6:23 KJV). When a person receives Christ as his Savior by accepting God's gift, at that moment he becomes born again.

It is so easy that a child can do it, but it can be difficult to admit that we cannot do it on our own. Jesus said that in order to enter the kingdom of heaven, a person must be willing to humble himself as a child, and only then will God receive him (see Matthew 18:3).

What about you? Have you done this? Have you been born again? If you want to be born again, we offer this prayer as an example of what you might pray: *Lord Jesus, I know that I am a sinner. I realize that I can't make it on my own. Thank You for dying for me. Right at this moment, the best way I know how, I trust You as my Savior and Lord, in Jesus' name. Amen.*

One important thing to note is that it is not the reciting of the above words that makes the difference. There is nothing magical in them; anyone can repeat a sentence. It is the attitude of your heart and your desire when you pray and trust Christ that makes the difference.

Excerpts taken from *Answers to Tough Questions Skeptics Ask About the Christian Faith* by Josh McDowell and Don Stewart (Carol Stream, IL: Tyndale House Publishers, 1980).

APPENDIX C

THE RESURRECTION OF JESUS[86]

By William Lane Craig (reprinted with permission)

SUMMARY

Examines the historical grounds for belief in Jesus' resurrection, focusing on the empty tomb, His post-mortem appearances, and the origin of the disciples' belief in His resurrection.

I spoke recently at a major Canadian university on the existence of God. After my talk, one slightly irate co-ed wrote on her comment card, "I was with you until you got to the stuff about Jesus. God is not the Christian God!"

This attitude is all too typical today. Most people are happy to agree that God exists; but in our pluralistic society it has become politically incorrect to claim that God has revealed Himself decisively in Jesus. What justification can Christians offer, in contrast to Hindus, Jews, and Muslims, for thinking that the Christian God is real?

The answer of the New Testament is: the resurrection of Jesus. "God will judge the world with justice by the man He has appointed. He has given proof of this to all men by raising him from the dead" (Acts 17:31). The resurrection is God's vindication of Jesus' radical personal claims to divine authority.

86. William Lane Craig, "The Resurrection of Jesus: Reasonable Faith," Reasonable Faith. Accessed March 3, 2021. https://www.reasonablefaith.org/writings/popular-writings/jesus-of-nazareth/the-resurrection-of-jesus/.

So how do we know that Jesus is risen from the dead? The Easter hymnwriter says, "You ask me how I know He lives? He lives within my heart!" This answer is perfectly appropriate on an individual level. But when Christians engage unbelievers in the public square—such as in "Letters to the Editor" of a local newspaper, on call-in programs on talk-radio, at PTA meetings, or even just in conversation with co-workers, then it's crucial that we be able to present objective evidence in support of our beliefs. Otherwise, our claims hold no more water than the assertions of anyone else claiming to have a private experience of God.

Fortunately, Christianity, as a religion rooted in history, makes claims that can in important measure be investigated historically. Suppose, then, that we approach the New Testament writings not as inspired Scripture, but merely as a collection of Greek documents coming down to us out of the first century, without any assumption as to their reliability other than the way we normally regard other sources of ancient history. We may be surprised to learn that the majority of New Testament critics investigating the gospels in this way accept the central facts undergirding the resurrection of Jesus. I want to emphasize that I am not talking about evangelical or conservative scholars only, but about the broad spectrum of New Testament critics who teach at secular universities and non-evangelical seminaries. Amazing as it may seem, most of them have come to regard as historical the basic facts which support the resurrection of Jesus. These facts are as follows:

FACT #1

After his crucifixion, Jesus was buried in a tomb by Joseph of Arimathea. This fact is highly significant because it means, contrary to radical critics like John Dominic Crossan of the Jesus Seminar, that the location of Jesus' burial site was known to Jew and Christian alike. In that case, the disciples could never have proclaimed His resurrection in Jerusalem if the tomb had not been empty. New Testament researchers have established this first fact on the basis of evidence such as the following:

1. Jesus' burial is attested in the very old tradition quoted by Paul in 1 Cor. 15:3–5:

> *For I delivered to you as of first importance what I also received: . . . that Christ died for our sins in accordance with the Scriptures, and that He was buried, and that He was raised on the third day in accordance with the Scriptures, and that He appeared to Cephas, then to the Twelve.*

Paul not only uses the typical rabbinical terms "received" and "delivered" with regard to the information he is passing on to the Corinthians, but vv. 3–5 are a highly stylized four-line formula filled with non-Pauline characteristics. This has convinced all scholars that Paul is, as he says, quoting from an old tradition which he himself received after becoming a Christian. This tradition probably goes back at least to Paul's fact-finding visit to Jerusalem around AD 36, when he spent two weeks with Cephas and James (Gal. 1:18). It thus dates to within five years after Jesus' death. So short a time span and such personal contact make it idle to talk of legend in this case.

2. The burial story is part of very old source material used by Mark in writing his gospel. The gospels tend to consist of brief snapshots of Jesus' life which are loosely connected and not always chronologically arranged. But when we come to the passion story, we do have one, smooth, continuously-running narrative. This suggests that the passion story was one of Mark's sources of information in writing his gospel. Now most scholars think Mark is already the earliest gospel, and Mark's source for Jesus' passion is, of course, even older. Comparison of the narratives of the four gospels shows that their accounts do not diverge from one another until *after* the burial. This implies that the burial account was part of the passion story. Again, its great age militates against its being legendary.

3. As a member of the Jewish court that condemned Jesus, Joseph of Arimathea is unlikely to be a Christian invention. There was strong resentment against the Jewish leadership for their role in the condemnation of Jesus (1 Thess. 2:15). It is therefore highly improbable that Christians would invent a member of the court that condemned Jesus who honors Jesus by giving him a proper burial instead of allowing him to be dispatched as a common criminal.

4. No other competing burial story exists. If the burial by Joseph were fictitious, then we would expect to find either some historical trace of what actually happened to Jesus' corpse or at least some competing legends. But all our sources are unanimous on Jesus' honorable interment by Joseph.

For these and other reasons, the majority of New Testament

critics concur that Jesus was buried in a tomb by Joseph of Arimathea. According to the late John A. T. Robinson of Cambridge University, the burial of Jesus in the tomb is "one of the earliest and best-attested facts about Jesus."[87]

FACT #2

On the Sunday following the crucifixion, Jesus' tomb was found empty by a group of his women followers. Among the reasons which have led most scholars to this conclusion are the following:

1. The empty tomb story is also part of the old passion source used by Mark. The passion source used by Mark did not end in death and defeat, but with the empty tomb story, which is grammatically of one piece with the burial story.

2. The old tradition cited by Paul in 1 Cor. 15:3–5 implies the fact of the empty tomb. For any first century Jew, to say that of a dead man "that He was buried and that He was raised" is to imply that a vacant grave was left behind. Moreover, the expression "on the third day" probably derives from the women's visit to the tomb on the third day, in Jewish reckoning, after the crucifixion. The four-line tradition cited by Paul summarizes both the gospel accounts and the early apostolic preaching (Acts 13:28–31); significantly, the third line of the tradition corresponds to the empty tomb story.

3. The story is simple and lacks signs of legendary embellishment. All one has to do to appreciate this point is to compare Mark's account with the wild legendary stories found in the second-century

87. John A. T. Robinson, *The Human Face of God* (Philadelphia: Westminster, 1973), 131.

apocryphal gospels, in which Jesus is seen coming out of the tomb with his head reaching up above the clouds and followed by a talking cross!

4. The fact that women's testimony was discounted in first century Palestine stands in favor of the women's role in discovering the empty tomb. According to Josephus, the testimony of women was regarded as so worthless that it could not even be admitted into a Jewish court of law. Any later legendary story would certainly have made male disciples discover the empty tomb.

5. The earliest Jewish allegation that the disciples had stolen Jesus' body (Matt. 28:15) shows that the body was in fact missing from the tomb. The earliest Jewish response to the disciples' proclamation, "He is risen from the dead!" was not to point to his occupied tomb and to laugh them off as fanatics, but to claim that they had taken away Jesus' body. Thus, we have evidence of the empty tomb from the very opponents of the early Christians.

One could go on, but I think enough has been said to indicate why, in the words of Jacob Kremer, an Austrian specialist in the resurrection, "By far most exegetes hold firmly to the reliability of the biblical statements concerning the empty tomb."[88]

FACT #3

On multiple occasions and under various circumstances, different individuals and groups of people experienced appearances of Jesus alive from the dead.

88. Jacob Kremer, *Die Osterevangelien—Geschichten um Geschichte* (Stuttgart: Katholisches Bibelwerk, 1977), 49–50.

This is a fact which is almost universally acknowledged among New Testament scholars, for the following reasons:

1. The list of eyewitnesses to Jesus' resurrection appearances which is quoted by Paul in 1 Cor. 15:5–7 guarantees that such appearances occurred. These included appearances to Peter (Cephas), the Twelve, the 500 brethren, and James.

2. The appearance traditions in the gospels provide multiple, independent attestation of these appearances. This is one of the most important marks of historicity. The appearance to Peter is independently attested by Luke, and the appearance to the Twelve by Luke and John. We also have independent witness to Galilean appearances in Mark, Matthew, and John, as well as to the women in Matthew and John.

3. Certain appearances have earmarks of historicity. For example, we have good evidence from the gospels that neither James nor any of Jesus' younger brothers believed in him during his lifetime. There is no reason to think that the early church would generate fictitious stories concerning the unbelief of Jesus' family had they been faithful followers all along. But it is indisputable that James and his brothers did become active Christian believers following Jesus' death. James was considered an apostle and eventually rose to the position of leadership of the Jerusalem church. According to the first century Jewish historian Josephus, James was martyred for his faith in Christ in the late AD 60s. Now most of us have brothers. What would it take to convince you that your brother is the Lord, such that you would be ready to die for that belief? Can there be any doubt this remarkable transformation in Jesus' younger brother took place because, in Paul's words, "then he appeared to James"?

Even Gerd Ludemann, the leading German critic of the resurrection, himself admits, "It may be taken as historically certain that Peter and the disciples had experiences after Jesus' death in which Jesus appeared to them as the risen Christ."[89]

FACT #4

The original disciples believed that Jesus was risen from the dead despite their having every predisposition to the contrary. Think of the situation the disciples faced after Jesus' crucifixion:

1. Their leader was dead. And Jews had no belief in a dying, much less rising, Messiah. The Messiah was supposed to throw off Israel's enemies (Rome) and re-establish a Davidic reign—not suffer the ignominious death of [a] criminal.

2. According to Jewish law, Jesus' execution as a criminal showed him out to be a heretic, a man literally under the curse of God (Deut. 21:23). The catastrophe of the crucifixion for the disciples was not simply that their Master was gone, but that the crucifixion showed, in effect, that the Pharisees had been right all along, that for three years they had been following a heretic, a man accursed by God!

3. Jewish beliefs about the afterlife precluded anyone's rising from the dead to glory and immortality before the general resurrection at the end of the world. All the disciples could do was to preserve their Master's tomb as a shrine where his bones could reside until that day when all of Israel's righteous dead would be raised by God to glory.

Despite all this, the original disciples believed in and were willing

89. Gerd Ludemann, *What Really Happened to Jesus?*, trans. John Bowden (Louisville, KY: Westminster John Knox Press, 1995), 80.

to go to their deaths for the fact of Jesus' resurrection. Luke Johnson, a New Testament scholar from Emory University, muses, "some sort of powerful, transformative experience is required to generate the sort of movement earliest Christianity was."[90] N. T. Wright, an eminent British scholar, concludes, "that is why, as a historian, I cannot explain the rise of early Christianity unless Jesus rose again, leaving an empty tomb behind him."[91]

In summary, there are four facts agreed upon by the majority of scholars who have written on these subjects which any adequate historical hypothesis must account for: Jesus' entombment by Joseph of Arimathea, the discovery of his empty tomb, his post-mortem appearances, and the origin of the disciples' belief in his resurrection.

Now the question is: what is the best explanation of these four facts? Most scholars probably remain agnostic about this question. But the Christian can maintain that the hypothesis that best explains these facts is "God raised Jesus from the dead."

In his book *Justifying Historical Descriptions*, historian C. B. McCullagh lists six tests which historians use in determining what is the best explanation for given historical facts.[92] The hypothesis "God raised Jesus from the dead" passes all these tests:

1. It has great *explanatory scope*: it explains why the tomb was found empty, why the disciples saw post-mortem appearances of Jesus, and why the Christian faith came into being.

2. It has great *explanatory power*: it explains why the body of Jesus

90. Luke Timothy Johnson, *The Real Jesus* (San Francisco: Harper San Francisco, 1996), 136.
91. N. T. Wright, "The New Unimproved Jesus," *Christianity Today* (September 13, 1993), 26.
92. C. Behan McCullagh, *Justifying Historical Descriptions* (Cambridge: Cambridge University Press, 1984), 19.

was gone, why people repeatedly saw Jesus alive despite his earlier public execution, and so forth.

3. It is *plausible*: given the historical context of Jesus' own unparalleled life and claims, the resurrection serves as divine confirmation of those radical claims.

4. It is *not ad hoc* or *contrived*: it requires only one additional hypothesis: that God exists. And even that needn't be an additional hypothesis if one already believes that God exists.

5. It is *in accord with accepted beliefs*. The hypothesis: "God raised Jesus from the dead" doesn't in any way conflict with the accepted belief that people don't rise *naturally* from the dead. The Christian accepts *that* belief as wholeheartedly as he accepts the hypothesis that God raised Jesus from the dead.

6. It *far outstrips any of its rival hypotheses in meeting conditions 1–5*. Down through history various alternative explanations of the facts have been offered; for example, the conspiracy hypothesis, the apparent death hypothesis, the hallucination hypothesis, and so forth. Such hypotheses have been almost universally rejected by contemporary scholarship. None of these naturalistic hypotheses succeeds in meeting the conditions as well as the resurrection hypothesis.

Now this puts the sceptical critic in a rather desperate situation. A few years ago I participated in a debate on the resurrection of Jesus with a professor at the University of California, Irvine. He had written his doctoral dissertation on the resurrection, and he was thoroughly familiar with the evidence. He could not deny the facts of Jesus' honorable burial, empty tomb, post-mortem appearances, and the origin of the disciples' belief in the resurrection. So his only recourse was to come up with some alternate explanation of those facts. And so he argued that Jesus of Nazareth had an unknown, identical twin brother, who was separated from him as an infant and grew up independently, but who came back to Jerusalem at the time of the crucifixion, stole Jesus' body out of the tomb, and presented himself to the disciples, who mistakenly inferred that Jesus was risen from the dead! Now I won't bother to go into how I went about refuting this theory. But I think the example is illustrative of the desperate lengths to which scepticism must go in order to refute the evidence for the resurrection of Jesus. Indeed, the evidence is so powerful that one of the world's leading Jewish theologians, the late Pinchas Lapide, who taught at Hebrew University in Israel, declared himself convinced on the basis of the evidence that the God of Israel raised Jesus of Nazareth from the dead![93]

The significance of the resurrection of Jesus lies in the fact that it is not just any old Joe Blow who has been raised from the dead, but Jesus of Nazareth, whose crucifixion was instigated by the Jewish leadership because of his blasphemous claims to divine authority. If this man has been raised from the dead, then the God whom he allegedly blasphemed has clearly vindicated his claims. In an age of religious relativism and pluralism, the resurrection of Jesus constitutes a solid rock on which Christians can take their stand for God's decisive self-revelation in Jesus.

93. Pinchas Lapide, *The Resurrection of Jesus*, trans. Wilhelm C. Linss (London: SPCK, 1983).

Appendix D

SCIENCE INCREASINGLY MAKES THE CASE FOR GOD[94]

By Eric Metaxas

In 1966 *Time* magazine ran a cover story asking: Is God Dead? Many have accepted the cultural narrative that he's obsolete—that as science progresses, there is less need for a "God" to explain the universe. Yet it turns out that the rumors of God's death were premature. More amazing is that the relatively recent case for his existence comes from a surprising place—science itself.

Here's the story: The same year *Time* featured the now-famous headline, the astronomer Carl Sagan announced that there were two important criteria for a planet to support life: The right kind of star, and a planet the right distance from that star. Given the roughly octillion—1 followed by 27 zeros—planets in the universe, there should have been about [a] septillion—1 followed by 24 zeros—planets capable of supporting life.

With such spectacular odds, the Search for Extraterrestrial Intelligence, a large, expensive collection of private and publicly funded projects launched in the 1960s, was sure to turn up something soon. Scientists listened with a vast radio telescopic network for signals that resembled coded intelligence and were not merely random.

94. . Reprinted with permission of the *Wall Street Journal*, Copyright © (2014) Dow Jones & Company, Inc. All Rights Reserved Worldwide. License number 4818931186951.

But as years passed, the silence from the rest of the universe was deafening. Congress defunded SETI in 1993, but the search continues with private funds. As of 2014, researchers have discovered precisely bubkis—0 followed by nothing.

What happened? As our knowledge of the universe increased, it became clear that there were far more factors necessary for life than Sagan supposed. His two parameters grew to 10 and then 20 and then 50, and so the number of potentially life-supporting planets decreased accordingly. The number dropped to a few thousand planets and kept on plummeting.

Even SETI proponents acknowledged the problem. Peter Schenkel wrote in a 2006 piece for *Skeptical Inquirer* magazine: "In light of new findings and insights, it seems appropriate to put excessive euphoria to rest. . . . We should quietly admit that the early estimates . . . may no longer be tenable."

As factors continued to be discovered, the number of possible planets hit zero, and kept going. In other words, the odds turned against any planet in the universe supporting life, including this one. Probability said that even we shouldn't be here.

Today there are more than 200 known parameters necessary for a planet to support life—every single one of which must be perfectly met, or the whole thing falls apart. Without a massive planet like Jupiter nearby, whose gravity will draw away asteroids, a thousand times as many would hit Earth's surface. The odds against life in the universe are simply astonishing.

Yet here we are, not only existing, but talking about existing. What can account for it? Can every one of those many parameters have been perfect by accident? At what point is it fair to admit that science suggests that we cannot be the result of random forces? Doesn't assuming that an intelligence created these perfect conditions require far less faith than believing that a life-sustaining Earth just happened to beat the inconceivable odds to come into being?

There's more. The fine-tuning necessary for life to exist on a planet is nothing compared with the fine-tuning required for the universe to exist at all. For example, astrophysicists now know that the values of the four fundamental forces—gravity, the electromagnetic force, and the "strong" and "weak" nuclear forces—were determined less than one millionth of a second after the big bang. Alter any one value and the universe could not exist. For instance, if the ratio between the nuclear strong force and the electromagnetic force had been off by the tiniest fraction of the tiniest fraction—by even one part in 100,000,000,000,000,000—then no stars could have ever formed at all. Feel free to gulp.

Multiply that single parameter by all the other necessary conditions, and the odds against the universe existing are so heart-stoppingly astronomical that the notion that it all "just happened" defies common sense. It would be like tossing a coin and having it come up heads 10 quintillion times in a row. Really?

Fred Hoyle, the astronomer who coined the term "big bang," said that his atheism was "greatly shaken" at these developments. He later wrote that "a common-sense interpretation of the facts suggests that a super-intellect has monkeyed with the physics, as well as with chemistry and biology. . . . The numbers one calculates from the facts seem to me so overwhelming as to put this conclusion almost beyond question."

Theoretical physicist Paul Davies has said that "the appearance of design is overwhelming," and Oxford professor Dr. John Lennox has said "the more we get to know about our universe, the more the hypothesis that there is a Creator . . . gains in credibility as the best explanation of why we are here."

The greatest miracle of all time, without any close seconds, is the universe. It is the miracle of all miracles, one that ineluctably points with the combined brightness of every star to something—or Someone—beyond itself.

BIBLIOGRAPHY

CHAPTER 1: IS BUSINESS A REAL CALLING, AND IF SO, IS IT AN IMPORTANT ONE?

Costa, Kenneth. *God at Work: Live Each Day with Purpose*. Nashville: W Publishing, 2016.

Guinness, Os. *The Call: Finding and Fulfilling God's Purpose for Your Life*. Nashville: W Publishing Group, 2018.

Warren, Rick. *The Purpose-Driven Life: What on Earth Am I Here For?* Grand Rapids: Zondervan, 2016.

CHAPTER 2: WOULD THE ELEPHANT IN THE ROOM PLEASE STAND UP?

Grudem, Wayne A. *Business for the Glory of God: The Bible's Teaching on the Moral Goodness of Business*. Wheaton, IL: Crossway Books, 2003.

Richards, Jay W. *Money, Greed, and God: 10th Anniversary Edition*. New York: HarperCollins, 2019.

CHAPTER 3: THE GREAT WHY

Stanley, Andy. *Irresistible: Reclaiming the New That Jesus Unleashed on the World*. Grand Rapids: Zondervan, 2018.

CHAPTER 4: THE GREATEST WHY

Ruthven, Jon. *On the Cessation of the Charismata: The Protestant Polemic on Post-Biblical Miracles*. Tulsa, OK: Word & Spirit Press, 2011.

CHAPTER 6: KNOW JESUS!

Stott, John W. *The Cross of Christ: 20th Anniversary Edition*. Nottingham, England: Inter-Varsity Press, 2006.

Tozer, A. W. *Knowledge of the Holy: The Attributes of God*. North Fort Myers, FL: Faithful Life Publishers, 2014.

CHAPTER 7: KNOW THAT THE BIBLE IS TRUSTWORTHY

Craig, William Lane. *Reasonable Faith: Christian Truth and Apologetics*. Wheaton, IL: Crossway Books, 2008.

Geisler, Norman L., and Thomas A. Howe. *The Big Book of Bible Difficulties*. Grand Rapids: Baker Books, 2008.

Geisler, Norman L., and William C. Roach. *Defending Inerrancy: Affirming the Accuracy of Scripture for a New Generation*. Grand Rapids: Baker Books, 2011.

Geisler, Norman L., and Frank Turek. *I Don't Have Enough Faith to Be an Atheist*. Wheaton, IL: Crossway Books, 2007.

Josephus, Flavius. *Josephus: The Complete Works*. Translated by William Whiston. Nashville: Thomas Nelson, Inc, 2004.

CHAPTER 8: KNOW THAT THE RESURRECTION OF JESUS IS ROOTED IN HISTORY

Copan, Paul, and Ronald Keith Tacelli, eds. *Jesus' Resurrection: Fact or Figment?: A Debate Between William Lane Craig and Gerd Lüdemann*. Downers Grove, IL: InterVarsity Press, 2000.

Habermas, Gary R., and Mike Licona. *The Case for the Resurrection of Jesus*. Grand Rapids: Kregel Publications, 2004.

Morison, Frank. *Who Moved the Stone?*. London: Faber & Faber, 1958.

CHAPTER 9: KNOW THAT FAITH IN GOD IS COMPATIBLE WITH MODERN SCIENCE

Lennox, John C. *God's Undertaker: Has Science Buried God?* Oxford, England: Lion Books, 2020.

Lennox, John C. *Gunning for God: Why the New Atheists Are Missing the Target*. Oxford, England: Lion, 2011.

Meyer, Stephen C. *Darwin's Doubt: The Explosive Origin of Animal Life and the Case for Intelligent Design*. New York: HarperOne, 2014.

Meyer, Stephen C. *The Return of the God Hypothesis: Compelling Scientific Evidence for the Existence of God*. New York: HarperOne, 2020.

Meyer, Stephen C. *Signature in the Cell: DNA and the Evidence for Intelligent Design*. New York: HarperOne, 2010.

Ross, Hugh. *Why the Universe Is the Way It Is*. Grand Rapids: Gardners Books, 2008.

CHAPTER 10: KNOW THAT ALL RELIGIONS CAN BE FALSE, BUT ONLY ONE CAN BE TRUE

Geisler, Norman L., and William D. Watkins. *Worlds Apart: A Handbook on World Views*. Eugene, OR: Wipf and Stock Publishers, 2003.

Murray, Abdu. *Grand Central Question: Answering the Critical Concerns of the Major Worldviews*. Downers Grove, IL: InterVarsity Press, 2014.

Sire, James W. *The Universe Next Door: A Guidebook to World Views*. Downers Grove, IL: InterVarsity Press, 1998.

ACKNOWLEDGMENTS

I am deeply grateful to the many people who have helped bring this book to the point of publication. Without their encouragement, insights, and guidance, this book would likely not have happened.

First and foremost, I am very thankful to my wife, Mary. Beyond her pivotal role in my coming to faith, Mary's input regarding the manuscript helped immensely. As a result of her constructive comments, I made several additions and deletions. In many ways, she is the co-author of this book. While I was generally "the face" in the business units I led, Mary was always present behind the scenes with helpful advice and encouragement. While some aspects of business can seem complex, it is generally not rocket science. At the end of the day, dealing effectively with other people is the biggest critical success factor. And Mary's advice in this area was always invaluable.

The original idea of writing this or any book wasn't mine. Indeed, I resisted the idea. However, many marketplace leaders engaged in LeaderImpact encouraged me to write a book as a result of reading my weekly blogs over the course of my time with the organization. I am deeply thankful for their encouragement since I ultimately concluded that the Lord was speaking to me through them.

Of course, there's a big difference between writing competently and creating a book people will actually read! I am indebted to the Fedd Agency for helping me convert my passion for helping marketplace leaders explore the relevance of faith in God into a coherent book. My first thanks go to Esther Fedorkevich, founder of the

Fedd Agency, for believing in me and my message. Thanks also to Tori Thacher, senior editor, and her team. The final product is a big improvement over the initial manuscript submitted for their input!

Thanks also to the many accomplished leaders who endorsed the book. In one sense, these messengers are the message. Many have enjoyed significant business success without compromising their faith. Indeed, it could be argued that they prospered in their leadership roles because they were faithful in responding to Jesus' call on their lives.

Finally, I am eternally grateful to my Lord and Savior, Jesus Christ. He is the ultimate inspiration behind *More Than Your Business Card*.

ABOUT THE AUTHOR

Garth Jestley earned his MBA from Richard Ivey School of Business in London Ontario and BSc from University of British Columbia and holds the Chartered Financial Analyst designation. Over the course of his business career, he has held many senior leadership positions including vice president of both Citibank and Bank of Montreal and CEO of Middlefield Group's core investment management business.

After stepping back from his full-time duties at Middlefield in 2012, Garth assumed the role of Executive Director of LeaderImpact for several years. The mission of LeaderImpact is to help marketplace leaders across Canada and around the world explore the relevance of faith in God in their professional and personal lives.

Garth and his wife Mary are involved in various church leadership roles and enjoy spending time with their children and grandchildren.